Modern Britain
1929-1939

Edited by
JAMES PETO AND DONNA LOVEDAY

Commissioning editor
ALAN POWERS

The Design Museum's *Modern Britain 1929–1939* exhibition,
20 January – 6 June 1999, was sponsored by Bacon & Woodrow.
Celebrating its 75th anniversary, the firm is the largest
independent partnership of actuaries and consultants in Europe.
St Olaf House, on the south bank of the Thames, designed by
H S Goodhart-Rendel 1929–31, is Bacon & Woodrow's
London headquarters and is a fine example of early
Modern construction methods in Britain.

75 years of financial foresight 1924-99

BACON & WOODROW

Contributors

Professor Andrew Causey is Senior Lecturer in Art History
at the University of Manchester.

Dr Judith Collins is the Curator of the Modern Collection
at the Tate Gallery.

Jane Fraser is Keeper of Decorative Arts
at the Harris Museum and Art Gallery, Preston.

John R Gold is Professor of Urban Geography
at Oxford Brookes University and is the author
of *The Experience of Modernism*.

Alastair Grieve is Reader in the History of Art
at the University of East Anglia.

Jeremy Myerson is Director of the Helen Hamlyn
Research Centre at the Royal College of Art, London.

Liz Paul is Curator of Art
at Manchester City Art Galleries.

Alan Powers is a freelance historian specialising
in twentieth century British Art and Design.

Jeremy Rewse-Davies is Head of Design at London Transport.

Acknowledgments

The Design Museum would like to thank especially the following individuals for
their invaluable advice and support during the planning of this exhibition:

Alan Powers and Judith Collins who
acted as curatorial advisers to the
exhibition.

Foster & Partners

Per Arnoldi

Sutton Vane Associates

Ou Baholyodhin

Malcolm Bailey

Charlotte Benton

Heather Butler

Andrew Causey

Richard Chamberlain

Trevor Chinn

Caroline Collier

Robert Elwall

Anita Feldman Bennet

Hannah Ford

Jane Fraser

Sharon Gayter

John Gold

Richard Green

Sarah Gretton

Alastair Grieve

Jane Hamlyn

Michael Harrison

Elain Harwood

Charles Hind

Lesley Hoskins

The Jackson Charitable Trust

Annely Juda

Sue Kerry

Jonathan Makepeace

Harriet McKay

Andrew Mead

David Mitchinson

Andrew Murray

Jeremy Myerson

Saskia Partington

Liz Paul

Annette Ratuszniak

Geoffrey Rayner

Jeremy Rewse-Davis

John Riddy

Ian Rogerson

Barley Roscoe

David Rosenberg

Cathy Ross

Jeffrey Salmon

Veronica Sekules

Paul Simms

Nick Walker

Nigel Wilkins

Hilary Williams

Erez Yardeni

The Design Museum would like to thank the following individuals and organisations who have lent artefacts to the exhibition:

The Architectural Press

Armley Mills Industrial Museum

The Chairman and Board of Governors of the BBC

Lady Bliss

Bexhill Museum

Dave Bonsall

Sir Alan Bowness

British Architectural Library, RIBA

Broadfield House Glass Museum

The Trustees of the British Museum

Hugh Carey

Cheltenham Museum and Art Gallery

Laura Cohn

The Dartington Hall Trust

De la Warr Pavilion, Bexhill-on-Sea (Rother District Council)

Frith Street Gallery

The Geffrye Museum

The Gordon Russell Trust

Government Art Collection

Mary Greensted

The Henry Moore Foundation

Holburne Museum

Impington Village College

Irish Architectural Archive (McGrath Collection)

Kettle's Yard, University of Cambridge

Leeds City Art Gallery

London Transport Museum

Sasha Lubetkin

Manchester City Art Gallery, Industrial Art Collection

Middlesex University, Silver Studio Collection

Warren and Victoria Miro

Andrew Murray

National Museum and Gallery, Cardiff

The National Trust, Willow Road

Pallant House Gallery (Kearley Bequest)

The Parchon Trust, De la Warr Pavilion, Bexhill-on-Sea

Penthouse, Highpoint

The Pier Gallery Collection

Alan Powers

Paul and Karen Rennie Collection

Stephen Rosenberg

The Royal Commission on the Historical Monuments of England, National Monuments Record

Salisbury Library and Galleries

Jeffrey Salmon

The Shell-Mex and BP Advertising Archive

The Shell Art Collection

Elizabeth Skelton

W Summers

Target Gallery, London

The Trustees of the Tate Gallery

University of Central England

University of East Anglia Collection

University of Wales, Bangor

Warner Fabrics plc

Allan Warren

The Wedgwood Museum

Whitworth Art Gallery, University of Manchester

York City Art Gallery

and all other contributors to the exhibition who wish to remain anonymous

The works illustrated on pages 36, 76 and 77 are reproduced by permission of the Henry Moore Foundation. The Design Museum would like to thank the lenders who have supplied photographs and to acknowledge the following photographers:

Michael Brandon-Jones

Michael Furze

Jefferson Smith

John Riddy

Contents

Foreword

SIR NORMAN FOSTER

If you had asked me as a teenager to name a modern British building, I would probably have pointed to the *Daily Express* building in Great Ancoats Street, Manchester; but I would not have been able to tell you that it was engineered by Sir Owen Williams and dated back to 1939, or very much else about it.

As a student, my imagination was fired first by two architects: Le Corbusier and Frank Lloyd Wright. I was thrilled to discover Corb's *Towards a New Architecture* where images of architecture and machines were juxtaposed. Wright's architecture, seen through the pages of Henry-Russell Hitchcock's *In the Nature of Materials,* seemed to belong to a far more remote fantasy world.

It is significant that, as a young architect, my first inspirations came from abroad – Europe and the United States – and only later from the Modernist buildings I began to discover closer to home. For architects practising in Britain in the 1930s, and for others involved in the visual arts generally at that time, the experience would have been very similar.

For example, Hitchcock and Johnson selected only two English buildings – Joseph Emberton's Royal Corinthian Yacht Club and Connell, Ward and Lucas's house at Amersham – for inclusion in their seminal 1932 International Style Exhibition at the Museum of Modern Art in New York, which was dominated by architecture from Germany, France, Scandinavia and the United States. You might argue that they could have searched harder, but if you look down a list of the buildings we now regard as canonic in the development of British Modernism – Finsbury Health Centre, the De la Warr Pavilion, Impington Village College – you find that they were, almost without exception, designed by European émigrés; sometimes they teamed up with Englishmen, but often they worked alone.

I believe it is not overstating the case that Modernism only really arrived in Britain with these émigrés. Architects such as Berthold

Lubetkin, Eric Mendelsohn, Marcel Breuer and Walter Gropius, who had pioneered Modernism in Europe, brought with them a pure strain of what had hitherto in Britain been a hybrid, even decorative style. Many of these émigrés, of course, moved on to the United States, and in most cases established careers in American universities where they influenced the next generation of architects.

My own story is picked up here again. After Manchester, a Henry fellowship allowed me to study for a master's degree at Yale, where Chermayeff became one of my tutors. Here I was, a young English architect, travelling to the United States in the early 1960s to benefit from an architectural education system whose roots had been torn up and transplanted nearly 30 years earlier. The irony of the situation was not lost on me.

Some critics would argue that Modernism has long become just another historic movement. But in my view that would be to forget the social idealism of its founders as well as their belief in technology as one of the keys to the future. The death of modern architecture was first predicted in the mid-1960s – just as I was starting to practice in England – and its obituaries began to appear ten years later. Despite such gloomy predictions, however, the Modern Movement in Britain, now in a more mature phase, has never been healthier or more vigorous. Along with this renewed energy has come an increasingly international focus. Architects and artists now cross borders to exhibit and build in a way that their counterparts in the 1930s would not have considered possible. For this, I would suggest, we owe those pioneering émigrés a special vote of thanks.

Introduction

Writing in 1933, the art historian and polemicist Herbert Read identified:

There have been revolutions in the history of art before today. There is a revolution with every new generation, and periodically, every century or so, we get a wider or deeper change of sensibility which is recognised as a period – the Trecento, *the* Quattrocento, *the Baroque, the Rococo, the Romantic, the Impressionist, and so on. But I do think we can already discern a difference in kind in the contemporary revolution; it is not so much a revolution, which implies a turning over, even a turning back, but rather a break up, a devolution, some would say a dissolution. Its character is catastrophic.*[1]

The break up or dissolution to which Herbert Read referred was the birth of the Modern Movement – an abrupt break with tradition which in the field of the visual arts Read identified in the impact of such painters as Gauguin and Van Gogh, but which was manifest at the turn of the century in all fields of social, scientific, political and philosophical endeavour, from Verlaine to Einstein. The 'catastrophic' nature of this dissolution was even to rock the Cambridge college of C S Lewis who, in his inaugural lecture of 1954, stated: 'I do not think that any previous age produced work which was, in its own time, as shatteringly and bewilderingly new as that of the Cubists, the Dadaists, the Surrealists, and Picasso has been in ours.'[2]

He could well have included the new architecture of Le Corbusier, Mies van der Rohe and Gropius, or the furniture experiments of Rietveld and Breuer.

When precisely the first tremors of the Modern Movement were felt is still a matter of research and debate, occupying the minds of many cultural seismologists. For that very Modern British novelist, Virginia Woolf, the birth of the Modern Movement in Britain can instantly be dated: 1910 – London's first post-Impressionist exhibition. Whilst

Notes

1 *Art Now*, London, 1933, revised edition 1960.
2 *De Descriptione Temporum: An Inaugural Lecture*, Cambridge, 1955.

13

attempts to pinpoint the precise moment of 'dissolution' abound, the Design Museum's exhibition on 'Modern Britain' chooses not to focus on a specific 'Year Zero' but rather to examine the decade preceding the Second World War.

However the key concern of the Design Museum's exhibition, *Modern Britain 1929–1939*, rests not solely in the timing of the earthquake, nor indeed in reading what point it registered on the Richter scale, but in identifying the continental plates that were affected by it. Can one talk about such a phenomenon as Modern *Britain*? Did Britain experience Modernism? What is unquestionable is the existence of a Modern movement in Britain in the visual and literary arts. Henry Moore, Barbara Hepworth, Paul Nash and Ben Nicholson present a modern vision in Britain, while Virginia Woolf and D H Lawrence, and English-speaking and domiciled novelists and poets, Conrad and Eliot, clearly belie the notion that somehow Modernism failed to touch the intellectual temper of the country. Nor is it possible to denigrate British scientific achievements of the period, achievements which were noted by and had a profound impact upon the cultural landscape of the period: in 1932 Chadwick discovered a new fundamental particle, the neutron, a discovery which was to lead directly to nuclear fission. In

Lubetkin and Tecton, Finsbury Health Centre, 1938. Exhibition panel.
British Architectural Library, RIBA, London.

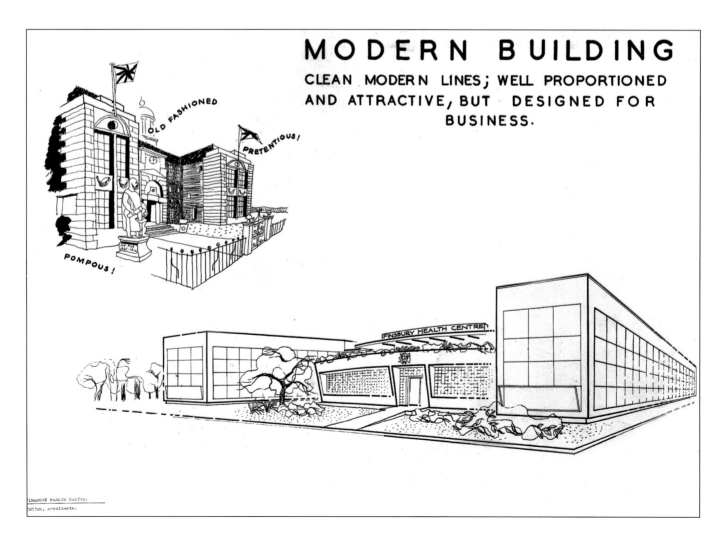

Paul Nash, *Dead Spring*, 1929. Oil on canvas.
Kearley Bequest, Pallant House Gallery.

the same year, J D Cockroft's and E T S Walton's 'smashing of the atom', which disproved the indivisibility of the atom, represented a turning point in man's understanding of structure. But were similar achievements happening in the world of man-man structures? Was there a Modern Britain in architecture and design?

In order to answer that question, one has to understand that one of the defining characteristics of Modernism is its wide geographical spread and its multiple nationality. Here was a movement which cut across boundaries, art forms, and at times, political sensibilities. Yet in each of the contributing countries there is a specific cultural inheritance (as Judith Collins's essay so fascinatingly unearths on page 69) and a peculiar set of social and political tensions which impose distinctly national emphases upon Modernism and leave any account which relies on a single national perspective misleadingly impartial.

Britain, of course, had a design avant-garde before the arrival of the émigrés Ernö Goldfinger, Marcel Breuer or Eric Mendelsohn in the 1920s and 1930s. It had its early Modern exponents in the late nineteenth century in the form of Christopher Dresser and C F A Voysey (although Voysey would have loathed the description), and witnessed a peculiar flowering of indigenous artistic and design talent during the period 1929–39, as the following essays demon-

Maxwell Fry, Miramonte, 1937.
Photograph: Architectural Press.

strate. Britain had its modern architects and designers: Wells Coates, Maxwell Fry, F R S Yorke, and Owen Williams. It had its patrons and commissioners of Modernism, perhaps not in quite in the league of a Truus Schröder, but in the Elmhirsts of Dartington, whose espousal of the modern nevertheless translated enduringly into the field of progressive secondary education, or the entrepreneur, Jack Pritchard, of Isokon. But, as Graham Sutherland's painting *Entrance*

to a Lane (1939) suggests, positioned symbolically at the close of the Design Museum's exhibition, the approach of a second world war was to starve the expressions of Modernist debate in Britain, leaving one only to speculate what the British equivalent of the house at New Canaan or the Harvard Graduate Center might have been had Breuer and Gropius not moved on to the United States.

What the Design Museum's exhibition and the following essays, I hope, reveal is that those seismic stirrings which shook Continental Europe at the turn of this century were also felt in Britain: there was conscious emulation of things European, there was genuine symbiosis, but there was also a peculiarly *British* response to the Modern.

DR PAUL THOMPSON
DIRECTOR, DESIGN MUSEUM
JANUARY 1999

H S Goodhart-Rendel, Hay's Wharf,
Lift shaft, 1932.
Photograph: Architectural Press.

The Search for a New Reality

ALAN POWERS

'So little divided us then, the architects, the artists, the philosophers, the engineers, even the industrialists who were members of this society, drawing together in difficult days when Welsh miners sang their lamenting songs for bread along the gutter of Victoria Street and Ramsay MacDonald failed finally to charm.'[1] In old age, Maxwell Fry looked back on the 1930s, as did many of his contemporaries, as a distinct and special period of unity in the arts and culture in Britain.

In 1979, when the Arts Council presented its *Thirties* exhibition at the Hayward Gallery, Fry's image of a 'heroic period' of British Modernism was replaced by a pluralism, including the other styles and modes of the decade. With a further 20 years' hindsight, the Modernist project of the 1930s describes a coherent enterprise which can be represented as a triple association between art, industry and the politics of the Left, each part being necessary to the others. This triadic grouping had little logical substance, but we cannot get inside the mind of the period without understanding why it mattered so much, even while its logical inadequacy led to its eventual abandonment as a complete system.

The First World War, rather than initiating Modernism in Britain as happened in almost every other European country, almost succeeded in killing what little existed of it before. Conservative tendencies were exaggerated by the inability to address the structural problems of British society, with its low level of investment in industrial modernisation and education, the reliance on the Empire to compensate for a weakening national economy and the loss of direction in the politics of the labour movement, even during its first brief period of government. In the arts, the result was a choice between hedonism and despair.

When the effects of the Wall Street Crash were felt, the awaited signal for real change was heard. Britain returned to the Gold

Notes

[1] Maxwell Fry, *Autobiographical Sketches*, London, 1975, p.137.

[2] Dmitri Mirsky, *The Intelligentsia of Great Britain*, London, 1935, p.39.

Standard in 1925, symbolising the desire to recreate the world as it was before 1914. The abandonment of the Gold Standard by the National Government in September 1931 was the defining moment of change in the wake of the Wall Street Crash. As Dmitri Mirsky wrote in *The Intelligentsia of Great Britain* in 1935:

Nineteen hundred and thirty-one was a year of marvels in the history of British capitalism. The fall of the pound, one of the chief weapons of power over the outside world, class struggles which were particularly ominous, because it was rumoured that the 'armed forces of His Majesty' had taken part in them, the first time since the eighteenth century (I think of [the 1931 naval mutiny at] Invergordon) and the institution of a dictatorship which however well got up in parliamentary robes was obvious to all, all this forced the intelligentsia of Great Britain to look face to face into historical realities from which there was no escaping . . . The principal result of 1931 for the intelligentsia was its return to politics. That revival of interest in politics was accompanied by an increased need for a world view, for a system. The purpose of this system was to save an intellectual from being isolated, to provide him with a group, to enable him to feel part of some greater whole, to elaborate a system of arguments to justify the aims of the whole, and in short to provide him with a key to the chaos, the so puzzling confusion into which reality seemed to have moved.[2]

Modernism, defined as the conscious desire to engage through culture with the reality of life following the process of social and economic modernisation, only broke through in Britain during the political upheaval of the early 1930s, having been deferred for a hundred years. As Mirsky indicates, it was a traumatic process brought about by extreme external pressures which obliged art to take a political standpoint.

The start date for English Modernism as a visual phenomenon predates the economic crisis. High and Over, Amersham, by Amyas Connell, was begun in 1929, Joseph Emberton's Olympia facade in 1930, and even H S Goodhart-Rendel, representing intelligent conservatism, radically revised his existing designs for Hay's Wharf in the same year. Raymond McGrath's mirror and glass interiors at Finella, Cambridge, for Mansfield Forbes, 1928–9, are significant as much for the people who met there as for their unusual quality as narrative symbolic Modernism. These examples belonged to a more innocent world than the one conjured by W H Auden in his first major publication, *Poems,* 1930. His vision of a sick country, with its lawless northlands of industrial devastation, in the 'charade' *Paid on Both Sides*, established the character of 'Auden Country'. Writers on social questions shared Auden's sense of the hopelessness of doing anything about it, short of a post-industrial 'greening'. At the end of his series in *The Listener*, 'Britain and the Modern World Order', 1932, Arnold Toynbee declared that: 'It looks at this moment as though our world order, as we know it, were more likely to dis-

Amyas Connell
High and Over, Amersham, 1929-31.
Photograph: British Architectural Library,
RIBA, London.

integrate and perish than to survive and grow . . . perhaps we are destined to revert to something like the material conditions of the pre-industrial age.'[3] Sir Evelyn Wrench, in the mood of the time that admired Italian Fascism, envisioned 'a Peace Army in Great Britain to pull down the slums in our big cities, build public baths on the Continental scale, to drain our waste land, and to make Great Britain a better and happier country than it is now'.[4]

Auden also cultivated an ironic affection for Fascism in *The Orators*, 1932, but in his densely-written sonnet about psychoanalysis, *Sir, no man's enemy* at the end of *Poems*, 1930, he closes with the line: 'Look shining at new styles of architecture, a change of heart.' Here, architecture was the metaphor for all constructive change, forcing a confrontation between the inner world of the psyche and the outer world of politics and affairs. Perhaps more clearly than architects themselves, Auden saw that what needed reforming in architecture sprang from a deeper level of social malaise: 'If our pulses were not confused by the rush of our age, there would be no need for Ye Olde Tea Shoppes.'[5]

Paul Nash's *Dead Spring*, 1929, also projected the unresolved spiritual crisis of a war veteran. It is an image to pair with T S Eliot's *The Waste Land*, 1922, in what George Orwell described as 'an age of eagles and of crumpets, facile despairs, backyard Hamlets, cheap return tickets to the end of night'.[6] Auden and his cohort of fellow poets, public-school educated, too young to have been in the war, engaged in political theatre, critical journalism and documentary film as well as poetry. In the despair of a situation so bad that the old expedients no longer covered over the cracks, the sense of a dead spring lasting ever since 1918 was changed when art discovered its social mission. Because design served direct needs, and might also contribute to healing the national malaise, Auden's contemporaries in architecture, lacking the opportunity to build, took any work they could get in industrial design, interiors, films and other areas, resulting in a diffusion of ideas from architecture into neighbouring fields. R D Russell came from his training at the Architectural Association to bring a Modern aesthetic and industrial production methods to Gordon Russell Ltd, his brother's craft-based firm in the Cotswolds.

The period from 1930 to 1934 was a time of intense discussion about all aspects of national life. Radio broadcasts, printed in *The Listener*, assessed the changing situation in Europe and Britain's role in the world. Design became a subject of public discussion for the first time, with a series of broadcasts, 'Design in Modern Life', in August 1933 when the interiors of Broadcasting House were still among the few British examples available as illustrations. *The Listener's* leader on the Gorrell Report on Art and Industry in 1932 praised its recognition that 'the present unsatisfactory relations of art and industry

[3] Arnold Toynbee, 'The International Landscape', *The Listener*, 6 July 1932, p.27.

[4] Sir Evelyn Wrench, 'The Need for a New Patriotism', *The Listener*, 16 November 1932, p.695.

[5] W H Auden, 'What is Wrong with Architecture?', *Architectural Review*, August 1933, p.66.

[6] George Orwell, 'Inside the Whale' (first published 1940) in *The Collected Essays, Journalism and Letters of George Orwell, Volume1, An Age Like This, 1920–40*, Harmondsworth,1970, p.559.

[7] 'Art and Industry', *The Listener*, 1 June 1932, p.780.

[8] Stephen Tallents, *The Projection of England*, London, 1932, p.35.

[9] Noel Carrington, *Design*, London, 1935, p.72.

are due to no superficial difficulties that can be smoothed away with a little mutual good will, but that they are grounded deep in our national life and can only be amended by a change of mind in the whole community'.[7] Design was thus poised to play a two-way role in resolving the crisis, both as the agent and outcome of social change and reform.

The role of design as an agent of change was most convincingly explained in *The Projection of England*, 1932, by Sir Stephen Tallents of the Empire Marketing Board, an institution whose modernity of outlook belied its name. Tallents called for a symbolic economy of information and expertise to replace the old one of primary goods and manufactures, almost post-industrial in its implications. Thus design would help to create a new international image of England, but would be less involved in the quantitative aspects of economics and production. Tallents, who is thought to have invented the term 'public relations', specially admired the German Pavilion at the Barcelona Exhibition of 1929, designed by Mies van der Rohe, calling it 'a gesture rather than a building', which seems to have symbolised his desire to shift from substance to sign.[8]

Whether or not the radical implications of Tallents's preference for propaganda over production was really understood, it conformed to a widespread desire to use design as part of the process of national reconstruction. There was an effort to find new versions of national identity, particularly in relation to other European cultures. The feeling of cultural inferiority was tempered by a more forgiving attitude of rediscovery and self-confidence, combined with a belief that, as Paul Nash put it, 'Going Modern and Being British' was not an impossible combination in the new economic circumstances. Noel Carrington wrote in 1935 that the wealth of Britain proved an obstacle to the reception of Modernism: 'in Germany the economic collapse made Design and Industry partners, whether they liked it or not . . . when our own turn came (though with nothing like the same severity) the same forces began to operate, and in one trade after another economy begat efficiency and thus cleared the way for the designer'.[9]

Going off the Gold Standard affected foreign exchange and reduced both the ability of the English to travel abroad and the ability to import goods or even exhibitions of foreign art. The Royal Academy opened its winter exhibition, *British Art*, in January 1934, in succession to a series on French, Italian, Spanish and Persian art, which prompted a discussion of the essential identity of British art. The restriction on foreign holidays, not unlike the similar stringency of the early 1990s, seems to have been a motive for rediscovering England, whether in literary journeys like those of J B Priestley or George Orwell, or in updating the image of England, particularly its seaside. The Shell Guide series was launched in June

Unknown Artist, Midland Hotel, Morecambe, 1933. Poster for LMS.
Paul and Karen Rennie Collection.

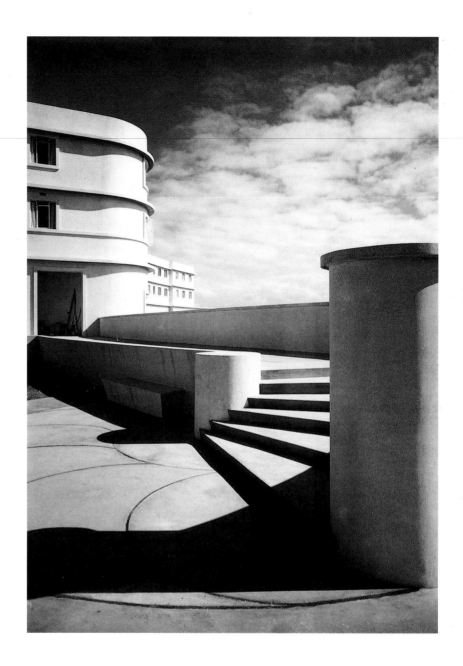

Oliver Hill, Midland Hotel,
Morecambe, 1930.
Photograph: Architectural Press.

Opposite page:
Erich Mendelsohn and Serge Chermayeff,
De la Warr Pavilion,
Bexhill-on-Sea, 1935.
Photograph: RCHME, Crown Copyright.

1934 with *Cornwall* by John Betjeman, whose visual presentation reflected the photography of the Bauhaus. The Midland Hotel, Morecambe, by Oliver Hill, was commissioned in 1932 by Ralph Glyn, the chairman of the London Midland and Scottish Railway, who was at the time Parliamentary Private Secretary to the Prime Minister, Ramsay MacDonald. The modern character hotel, which was completed in a year, appears to have been a symbolic gesture of optimism. The competition for the De la Warr Pavilion at Bexhill-on-Sea was announced in September 1933 and the most 'modern' design was picked from those submitted.

During the 1920s, attempts at reform, such as the government sponsored British Institute of Industrial Art and the voluntary Design and Industries Association (DIA), were limited in effect, partly because of lack of definition in their programme. The DIA included important spokesmen from industry, but still only from

small specialised firms like Dryad of Leicester and the Curwen Press. Reform within the DIA was led by Jack Pritchard with a programme of research and publication, briefly manifested in the journal *Design in Industry* in 1932. The idea of 'research' had a particular potency at the time, which the word may no longer carry. It suggested a kind of epistemological regrounding for art in the disciplines of science, with the possibility of impacting directly in a social sphere. Roger Fry's addendum to the Gorrell Report proposed 'Laboratories of Design'. J D Bernal, apart from being a distinguished research scientist in the field of crystallography, was a strong believer in the application of scientific thinking to practical problems and the increase in expenditure in industrial research and development for the national good.

The Twentieth Century Group, established in 1930, with Wells Coates, Serge Chermayeff and Raymond McGrath as its leading figures, was founded under the inspiration of Mansfield Forbes at Cambridge. Invisible to the public, it nonetheless formed an important, if short-lived, network. Up to this time, Coates and

Attributed to Raymond McGrath
Broadcasting House, Portland Place, London,
c. 1930: perspective view of proposed
Entrance Hall. Watercolour.
McGrath Collection, Irish Architectural Archive.

Chermayeff had only worked as designers of furniture, textiles and interiors, while McGrath had qualified as an architect but so far only produced the interiors for Forbes at Finella. Forbes's colleagues in the English faculty, like C K Ogden, I A Richards and William Empson, used the methodology of science as a way of dealing with the question of meaning in language, and Coates followed their lead in his paper 'Response to Tradition', 1932, which was counterposed in the *Architectural Review* with a defence of tradition by Sir Edwin Lutyens.

The Twentieth Century Group's programme was concerned with the promotion of Modernism through exhibitions. Chermayeff came with experience from the Modern Art Studio at Waring and Gillow of the need to 'sell' the idea of Modernism to a conservative British public, but believed that resistance could be overcome by adapt- ing continental models in the right way. The profession of ad-vertising, necessarily dealing with the symbolic aspects of the economy, found Modernism a perfect subject for its activity. Frank Pick of London Underground demonstrated how advertising could become part of a moral campaign of public service. Sir William Crawford, of Crawford's Advertising, not only commissioned the first Modern building in London from Frederick Etchells in 1929, but launched a campaign targeted on the business world under the title 'Design a Necessity'.

The three main members of the Twentieth Century Group were introduced, through Forbes's patronage, to the BBC and com- missioned to design interiors for the new Broadcasting House. Modern design, already a subject of discussion in radio, thus became physically incorporated into Sir John Reith's project of national education in the arts which tended to share his assumption of a top-down method of dissemination.

This produced a sense of remoteness between the artists and critics in London, whose thoughts have remained the main material for historians, and the actual context of industry for which Modernism was neither a crusade nor sheer opportunism. The major textile firms seem to have included a number of designs which we recognise as modern among other more traditional ones. Some of these were as adventurous and lively as anything by the 'named' designers, and give a stronger impression of vitality within the design culture of industry than the design reformers ever suggested. The idea of artistic reform as an external corrective to be applied from outside was also subverted by the recognition of 'design classics' such as Willow pattern, sporting clothes and men's clothes within the standard productions of industry and the 'trade' crafts, in Steen Eiler Rasmussen's exhibition and book of 1932, *Britisk Brugskunst*. When Nikolaus Pevsner conducted his *Inquiry into Industrial Art in England* between 1934 and 1936, he declared that

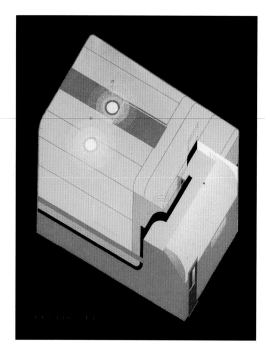

Raymond McGrath, BBC Dance Music
and Chamber Music Studio. Gouache.
British Architectural Library,
RIBA, London.

more than 90 per cent of English industrial products were artistically objectionable. It was clear that if good design was to be the outcome of social change, the transformation had not yet taken place. When Michael Farr wrote *Design in British Industry* as a successor survey in 1955, he estimated 80 to 90 per cent, so that the mid-term quantitative effects of design reform were very limited.

Paul Nash began an article on art and industry in 1932 with the line: 'A marriage has been arranged . . . and will shortly take place', which characterises the hoped-for union while admitting the unlikeli- ness of its success. What took place was more of a flirtation than a consummation. The tradition of artists criticising design on moral and patriotic grounds and proposing their own participation in reform goes back to Hogarth and *The Analysis of Beauty*, and could be extended through Ruskin and Morris to Roger Fry. Paul Nash was their successor in the 1930s. Of the group of painters, sculptors and architects that Nash brought together in 1933, he was the only one actively practising design on any scale, but hoped that the others would join him. The painter John Armstrong declared in his Unit One statement that it was not so much industry's need for art, but art's need for some grounding in reality that motivated him, which was an implied criticism of abstraction. Herbert Read's intro- duction to the Unit One book of 1934 which accompanied the group's only exhibition hardly mentions the subject of design, des- pite speaking of the artist's search for 'definite status and respon- sible function' in society. In terms of achieving a productive marriage between art and industry, Unit One must be deemed a failure. Kenneth Clark attacked abstraction in *The Listener* in 1935 for being too theoretical, but perhaps it was not theoretical enough for the tasks it attempted.

The Twentieth Century Group faded out in 1933, by which time Coates had begun to form MARS (Modern Architectural Research) as a successor; a more specifically architectural body which acted as a network and summarised the decade's activity in its exhibition at the New Burlington Galleries in 1938. The crossing over from one discipline to another was characteristic of the first stages of British Modernism, but although it worked for architects, the artists seemed to remain predominantly separate from industry, either (like Nash and Ben Nicholson) unable to accept compromises with production processes and markets or, like Edward McKnight Kauffer, losing their status in 'Fine Art' by absorption in 'Commercial Art'. With the development of a group of abstract painters in Britain by 1933, who also happened to need additional earnings, it was hoped to spark the kind of interchange between art and design that was known to have taken place in Russian Constructivism, De Stijl and the Bauhaus. Herbert Read's *Art and Industry*, 1934, begun while he was still working at the Victoria and Albert Museum, was, in the words of David Thistlewood, 'primarily a defence of the abstract artist, an individual . . . removed from ordinariness, whose researches into pure form were crucial both to the aesthetic and the commercial well-being of the community'.[10] In Read's words, 'abstract art' will occupy, in the future, a relationship to industrial design very similar to the relationship pure mathematics bears to the practical sciences. Probably such artists will be as rare and remote as pure mathematicians, but they will have an essential place in the aesthetic structure of the machine age.'[11] Read hoped again that his artist friends would play a part in Design Research Unit when he founded it with Marcus Brumwell of Stuart's Advertising in 1943, but it never really happened, apart from an ill-fated car body, designed by Naum Gabo. The post-war success of DRU was based on the emergence of professionally-oriented designers, although there was virtually no specific training for industrial design available until after the war. Practitioners in the arts tended to keep within their boundaries. Several of the designers who best illustrated the cross-over from art to design were outside the well-publicised circle of Unit One and the Hampstead avant-garde, for example, Denham Maclaren, who first studied painting in Paris before designing strikingly original modern furniture right at the beginning of the 1930s. Gerald Summers, whose plywood furniture has been described as 'arguably . . . Britain's single most important contribution to the evolution of modern furniture design',[12] came from an engineering background. It is clear that the talent of certain of the abstract artists and émigrés included the preparation of their own place in history as much as actual designing, and that the overall picture may be revised still further.

David Thistlewood identifies within Read's text a conflict between the conventional obeisance to Gropius and a personal preference for Moholy-Nagy's *The New Vision*, published in New York in 1932, with its more dynamic idea of new forms of perception, capable of disrupting the modern classicism of Gropius and introducing, however obliquely, concepts of pluralism which we can now identify as post-modern.[13] These tendencies within the 1930s are still contentious, probably because of the perceived need for Modernism to keep a united front, but it is possible to find within the evidence of the period a response to the criticisms subsequently voiced about a design ideology that was inhuman in its disregard for variety and choice and fanatical in its desire for imposing order and control. Ben Nicholson's white reliefs, which he began to carve in 1934 and continued until 1936, represent in one sense a high point of abstraction and internationalism, but also an exclusion of other forms of artistic language which even he soon found unsustainable.

Other countries which had experienced Modernism before Britain had to consider what to do next. In Germany, the Nazis brought their own solution to the problem by excluding Modernism from all but industrial buildings. In France after 1930, there was a strong

[10] David Thistlewood, *Herbert Read: formlessness and form*, London, 1984, p.108.

[11] Herbert Reed, *Art and Industry*, London, 1934, p.39.

[12] Martha Deese, 'Gerald Summers and Makers of Simple Furniture', *Journal of Design History*, 5: 3, 1992, pp. 183–206.

[13] See David Thistlewood, Herbert Reed: 'A New Vision of Art and Industry' in Herbert Reed, *A British View of World Art*, David Thistlewood and Benedict Read (eds), Leeds, 1993.

reaction against the idea of machine civilisation, perceptible even in the work of Le Corbusier, Ozenfant and Léger, as well as among more obviously conservative artists.[14] Coming from in-side the movement, this was potentially far more subversive than the rather ineffectual criticisms of Modernism in the English press, but while the development of Le Corbusier's work was eagerly followed and imitated in England, his change of di-rection seems not to have been fully grasped. A non-industrial Modernism, with a language of self-contradiction derived in part from Cubist collage, was now a possibility and had an in-stinctive appeal in England. In 1932, the exhibition *Modern Architecture* at MOMA established a benchmark for the purely aesthetic presentation, showing how the link between Modernism and social purpose could be broken. The change in approach following the dissolution of the Modernist triad can be seen in the difference between Lubetkin's Highpoint I (1933–35), a pure structure of monolithic concrete, and Highpoint II (1936–38), a framed structure with varied textures and colours and an overall symmetry. Ironically, the solution which looked less modern was demonstrably more practical in terms of construction and weathering, as well as being linguistically richer. Neither was this a one-off change in Lubetkin's work, which from this date became increasingly formal (or formalist, in the view of his sterner critics).

As the decade developed, Social Realism rather than Modernism became the approved style of the extreme Left. British architects did not see this in terms of a classical revival, although by the end of the decade buildings by modernists in-cluded regionalist characteristics such as timber, brick and pitched roofs. In painting, the foundation in 1937 of The School of Painting and Drawing (initially in Fitzroy Street, later in Euston Road, which gave it its popular name, The Euston Road School), with its programme of careful observation, was a direct result of William Coldstream's discussions with Auden when both were working for the GPO Film Unit in 1935. Having lost faith in the social value of abstract art,

. . . we turned our attention to Art
Upstairs in the Corner house, in the hall with the phallic pillars
And before the band had finished a pot-pourri from Wagner
We'd scrapped Significant Form and voted for Subject.[15]

Coldstream and another Euston Road painter, Graham Bell, joined in the work of Mass Observation, a movement of heterogeneous composition launched in 1937 by the painter and film-maker Humphrey Jennings, the poet Charles Madge, both sympathetic to Surrealism, and the anthropologist Tom Harrisson. Its first major publication was a survey of 12 May

[14] See Romy Golan, *Modernity and Nostalgia: art and politics in France between the wars*, New Haven and London, 1995.

[15] W H Auden and Louis MacNeice, *Letters from Iceland*, London, 1937, p.222.

Photomural, British Pavilion,
Paris 1937 Exhibition, Oliver Hill.
Photograph: Dell & Wainwright.

1937, the coronation day of King George VI, and its most characteristic product, the survey of Bolton, depicted generically as 'Worktown'.

1937 was a year of national self-examination. The coronation, coming after the abdication crisis of 1936, provided occasion for the anthropologically-minded to observe the persistence of rituals and traditions in popular culture. Manufacturers responded with commemorative goods of varying quality, but in examples like Keith Murray's glass and Eric Ravilious's Wedgwood Coronation mug, there was demonstrated a possible convergence between modern design and the kind of unpedigreed industrial production of a hundred years before. The coincidence of the centenary of Queen Victoria's coronation gave added emphasis to the existing nostalgia for the early nineteenth century and allowed for the creation of a category of 'good' industrial design from the past, quite different from Herbert Read's pure forms. In Paris, the creation of the Musée des Arts et Traditions Populaires in the new Palais du Trocadero elided left-wing and right-wing views of popular tradition and folk

PRESENTS

FOR PENCE

OR POUNDS

AT HEAL'S

196. TOTTENHAM COURT RD. LONDON. W.

art in a mixture that equally made no distinction between urban and rural.

The Paris Exhibition, which opened in June 1937, was a chance to see Britain in an international context. The British Pavilion, designed by Oliver Hill, was on a scale of Modernism below the Finnish, Czech and Swiss Pavilions, but above the French and Italian, and contrasted in its modest decency with the rhetorical German and Soviet ones. The pavilion followed a programme devised by Frank Pick, depicting Britain in South-Eastern guise as a country of weekend houses, middle-class sports, leather luggage and rural industries. Pick showed a surprising conservatism in some of his advice on the choice of artists and designers, vetoing Moholy-Nagy

William Lescaze, High Cross House, Dartington, 1932.
Photograph: The Dartington Hall Trust.

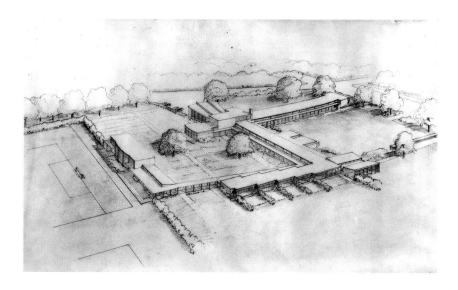

Walter Gropius and Maxwell Fry, Impington Village College, aerial perspective.
Pencil on tracing paper.
British Architectural Library, RIBA, London.

for so simple a task as arranging the photos in the silver section, writing to Oliver Hill: 'With regard to the photographs my only criticism of Mr Moholy Nagy is that he is a gentlemen with a modernistic tendency who produces pastiches of photographs of a surrealist type, and I am not at all clear that we should fall for this. It is international, or at least continental. The pavilion is a British Pavilion and Mr Moholy-Nagy has not got the British tradition I fear . . . Let us leave the continent to pursue their own tricks and go our own way traditionally.'[16] Pick's concept of British Tradition avoided 'period' style, so that furniture, if not by Isokon or Gerald Summers, was at least by Gordon Russell Ltd and Heals. This caution attracted criticism but the overall standard of the Pavilion was deemed infinitely superior to any previous effort and can be seen as a fulfilment of Stephen Tallents's idea of 'National Projection', particularly since the goods exhibited represented some of England's strongest exports. The inclusion of rural crafts was in line with the regionalist emphasis of the French sections, and even with the peasant costumes shown alongside Picasso's *Guernica* in the pavilion of the doomed Spanish Republic.

Opposite page:
Heals, *Presents: For Pence or Pounds.*
Poster 1930s. Courtesy of Heals Archive.

[16] Frank Pick, letter to Oliver Hill, 14 October 1936, British Architectural Library, Oliver Hill papers HiO/63/5.

William Lescaze, Country Club for Churston
Development Company, Churston Ferrers,
Devon (unexecuted), 1935. Watercolour.
The Dartington Hall Trust.

In 1933, Auden had exposed the shallowness of machine worship in
the Labour party newspaper, the *Daily Herald*: 'In theory machines
have made it possible for everyone to reach a standard of living
formerly unattainable even by the very rich. In practice they have so
far made a majority of mankind wretched and a minority unhappy,
spoiled children.'[17] In 'Letter to Lord Byron' in *Letters from Iceland*,
1936, he pronounced disbelief in the new world, seen merely as a
material production:

Preserve me from the Shape of Things to Be;
The high-grade posters at the public meeting
The influence of Art on Industry
The cinemas with perfect taste in seating.[18]

A review by Gavin Ewart of Auden's anthology, *The Poet's Tongue*,
1935, a collection arranged alphabetically, mixing 'fine' poetry with
ballads and nursery rhymes, praised his 'general iconoclastic
sanity'.[19]

The superior reality of the machine age was challenged by F R Leavis
and Denys Thompson in *Culture and Environment* in 1933, a teachers'
manual which showed how the ideas of progress and optimism pre-
vented 'intelligent and concerted remedial action' in society. Leavis
and Thompson hoped instead for the return of 'organic community', something which was being cultivated in Cambridge-shire
villages by the Village Colleges commissioned by Henry Morris, in
which schools were combined with community facilities, changing

[17] W H Auden ' A Poet Tells Us How To Be Masters
of the Machine', *Daily Herald*, 28 April 1933 in
Edward Mendelsohn (ed.) *W H Auden Prose
1926–38*, London, 1996.

[18] W H Auden and Louis MacNeice, *Letters from
Iceland*, p.51.

[19] Gavin Ewart, 'Poetry Itself', *New Verse*, August–
September 1935, p.20.

[20] Marion Richardson, 'Children's Drawings',
originally printed in London County Council's
Annual Report, 1936, Volume 5, Education,
reprinted in *Athene*, IV, Summer 1947, p.5.

[21] Marion Richardson, *Art and the Child*, London,
1948, p.56.

from the neo-Georgian of Sawston (1928) to the local authority modern of S E Urwin's designs for Bottisham and Linton, and finally Impington (1937–9) by Walter Gropius and Maxwell Fry. As with the experiment in rural regeneration at Dartington, begun by Leonard and Dorothy Elmhirst in 1926, the imagery of modern architecture was encouraged to take part in a project which was reformist rather than revolutionary, and designed to defend the values of small rural communities against those of the metropolis and American-based mass culture.

William Lescaze, 'Blacklers' Boarding House, Aller Park Junior School, Dartington Hall, 1932. Photograph: The Dartington Hall Trust.

While the education of the public was seen as the best means of achieving the wider aims of design reform, the actual teaching of art in schools was being transformed. Marion Richardson, whose work with children in Dudley was exhibited in 1920, spread a liberal but dedicated concern with art as a London County Council schools' inspector. In 1936 she wrote that children who are taught art properly, 'begin to be able to choose between the real and the sham because their own work, to themselves unmistakably sincere or otherwise, is giving them the touchstone'.[20] Richardson was responsible for a set of handwriting manuals based on pattern-making, published in 1935, and found that 'from these simple beginnings the London children extended their artistic vocabulary and developed a kind of

Walter Gropius, Drawing for proposed Open Air Theatre, Dartington Hall Gardens, 1935. Pencil on paper. The Dartington Hall Trust.

folk art'.[21] In a remote rural school in Wiltshire, Robin Tanner, himself a romantic ruralist etcher, was giving the same lesson of personal development and moral empowerment through art and craft, initially fiercely resisted by the teaching establishment. The craft revival, so readily written off in the wake of the Bauhaus, achieved a new life in the 1930s. The 'studio crafts', most typically represented by potters such as William Staite Murray and Bernard Leach, had a confidence that the survivors of the old Arts and Crafts Movement lacked. The Arts and Crafts Exhibition Society reinvented itself for a members' exhibition at the Dorland Hall in 1935, while an individual designer such as Enid Marx moved freely between designing

Ernö Goldfinger, House at Willow Road,
Hampstead, 1938-39.
Photograph: Architectural Press.

for machine production and block-printing fabrics by hand. Eric Gill, who continually restated his opposition to machine civilisation was the designer in 1926–7 of the Gill Sans type for the Monotype Corporation, one of the most enduring industrial designs of the period.

The growth of interest in Surrealism, culminating in the Surrealist Exhibition at the New Burlington Galleries in 1936, gave another focus to opposition within Modernism. Having rejected abstraction except as a means of design, Paul Nash found in it the fulfilment of his 1890s roots in Symbolism. Other artists used the movement to develop a more seriously anti-aesthetic attitude, diametrically opposed to the idealistic purity of the abstractionists, who retaliated with *Circle: an international survey of constructive art*, 1937, edited by Ben Nicholson, Naum Gabo and Leslie Martin. A surrealist architecture is hard to identify, apart from the commissions executed for Edward James, but the effect of surprising juxtapositions, with the poetic force of metaphor, is apparent in Lubetkin's later work and also in that of Ernö Goldfinger, a personal friend of many leading Parisian surrealists. Surrealism seems to have invigorated the perception of objects, whether in painting, fashion photography, *objets trouvés*, or in the increasingly sophisticated use of open grids and framing surrounds in architecture. This had some importance for design, requiring not so much a chorus of pure forms as a piquant conversation between dissimilar things.

The awakening to the pleasurable meanings of oxymoron and metaphor included a questioning of the nature of categories themselves. In 1935, Myfanwy Evans, who married John Piper in that year, started *Axis* as a small magazine of 'abstract' art, a term deliberately placed in inverted commas which, as the opening editorial explained, 'is used as a general name for the painting and

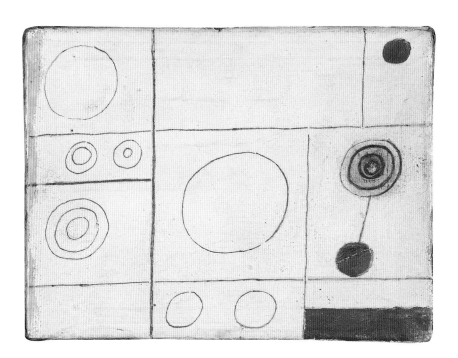

Ben Nicholson, *Abstract Box*, 1933.
Paint and pencil on cardboard box.
Kettle's Yard, University of Cambridge.

Ben Nicholson, Massine Ballet Study, 1934.
Oil on card.
Kettle's Yard, University of Cambridge.

sculpture of today that is not naturalistic, nor surrealist, nor purely decorative'.[22] The first number contained Geoffrey Grigson's 'Comment on England' based on the works illustrated, finding in them 'a small history of English ideas, English hesitancy, English error and English performance' and asking for the formalism of the Bloomsbury critics Clive Bell and Roger Fry to be replaced 'by no incapable tyranny of geometric and mechanical idealism, no permanent escape to the divided rectangle and the spokeless wheel'.[23] The vision of a role for the abstract artist in industry was never part of the *Axis* programme, but was replaced by a more inclusive vision of art itself. While the statements about art made by Nicholson, Hepworth and Moore (all of whom were admired by Grigson and the Pipers), in Unit One and elsewhere, referred to states of transcendental enlightenment, the writers in *Axis* differed from them in a more knockabout enjoyment of contradiction, which probably seemed a more appropriate response to the Spanish Civil War (1936–39) and the deteriorating situation in Europe.

Grigson's magazine *New Verse* (1934–38) served as an irritant for poetry in the same way that *Axis* did for art. Grigson and the Pipers made links between English culture and individualism, and were against group-forming or party-line politics. Grigson published a 'Commitment' special issue at the time of the Munich Crisis, writing: 'What we need now is not the fanatic but the critical moralist.'[24] The distaste for categories even included a desire to eliminate historical time as a barrier to the immediacy of experience, as Grigson wrote

[22] Editorial, *Axis*, 1, January 1938, p.3.
[23] Geoffrey Grigson, 'Comment on England', *Axis*, 1, January 1935, pp.8, 10.
[24] Geoffrey Grigson, 'Lonely, But Not Lonely Enough', *New Verse*, Autumn 1938, p.17.

Henry Moore, Maquette for *Recumbent Figure*,
1938. Bronze. Private Collection, London.
Photograph by Michael Furze.

in his joint article with Piper, 'England's Climate': 'There is no past.
There are no pictures painted "in the past", equally there is no
exclusive Fair Isle of the present. There is only a human instinct, a
being.'[25] The article was illustrated with reproductions of Constable,
Fuseli and Samuel Palmer, whose work had been rediscovered by
Graham Sutherland. Writing on 'A Trend in English Draughtsmanship', Sutherland also addressed the question of categories: 'It
is our wont, nowadays, in attempting to discuss the nature of things,
to make categories. This, however, is an imperfect method of
identification, and particularly so when we attempt to discuss the
nature of art; for the very qualities which we regard as being
especially characteristic of a particular type of art are, in fact, elusive,
and may be found to be a constituent of another type of art.'
Discussing the drawings of Henry Moore later in the same article,
Sutherland quotes the French neo-Thomist philosopher, Jacques
Maritain, to suggest that Moore's art is 'recomposing its peculiar
world with that poetic reality which resembles things in a far more

profound and mysterious way than any direct evocation could possibly do'. As Sutherland adds: 'We find Moore discovering one thing with the help of another, and by their resemblance making the unknown known.'[26] The awareness and enjoyment of contradiction expressed here is something which, with our hindsight, we can understand not just as a Romantic revival but as a precursor of post-Modernism, a consistent stage in the search for reality which preoccupied Moore and his fellow artists from their student days in the 1920s.

The Painter's Object, edited in 1937 by Myfanwy Evans, tried to go beyond the 'silly battle' of abstraction and Surrealism. John Piper's essay, 'Lost, a valuable object', suggested a third way, a return to an understanding of context: 'there is one striking similarity of the Surrealist and the abstract painter to the object: *they both have an absolute horror of it in its proper context*. The one thing neither of them would dream of painting is a tree standing in a field. For the tree standing in the field has practically no meaning at the moment for the painter. It is an ideal, not a reality.'[27]

Henry Moore, by refusing to take sides in the quarrel between abstractionists and surrealists, gave weight to the emerging sense of plurality. From 1938 onwards he also shared with Piper and Sutherland the patronage of Kenneth Clark, much to the disgust of Read and Nicholson who felt that Clark's influence was reactionary. If evidence was needed that the revision of Modernism was, as its advocates hoped, a cause for creativity rather than dissolution, then Serge Chermayeff's own house at Bentley Wood, Sussex, completed in 1938 and built with a white-painted timber frame, poised in the landscape beside Henry Moore's *Recumbent Figure* specially made for its terrace, and paintings by Piper and Nicholson inside, is the representative ensemble from the second half of the decade. The architecture was unusual in avoiding the typical box-like character of English modern houses by exposing the frame on the upper storey. Christopher Hussey reviewed the house in *Country Life* and found in it evidence that 'a new recognition has come that "abstract" architecture – that is, architecture designed purely to illustrate an intellectual thesis and without relation to setting or national tradition – is unsatisfying.'[28] In avoiding the more overt decorative Surrealism of Berthold Lubetkin's contemporary Highpoint II Penthouse, Chermayeff created a new direction in English architecture which remained an object of emulation after the war, when many other 1930s Modern buildings seemed as dated. John Summerson wrote in 1959, 'the house suppressed every vanity of "style" and merely touched the environment into consciousness of form; it was the most aristocratic English building of the decade'.[29] Moore's Hornton stone sculpture from Bentley Wood was bought by the Tate Gallery in 1939, the first example of his work to enter a public collection. He described it as 'the first figure in stone to be

[25] Geoffrey Grigson and John Piper, 'England's Climate', *Axis*, Autumn 1936, p.9.

[26] Graham Sutherland, 'A Trend in English Draughtsmanship', *Signature*, 3, July 1936, pp.7–13.

[27] John Piper, 'Lost, a valuable object', in Myfanwy Evans (ed.), *The Painter's Object*, London, 1937, p.70.

[28] Christopher Hussey, 'Bentley, near Halland, Sussex', *Country Life*, 26 October 1940, p.370.

[29] John Summerson, introduction to Trevor Dannatt's *Modern Architecture in Britain*, London, 1959, p.17.

substantially opened out'. The landscape at Bentley Wood was 'designed' chiefly through the removal of existing trees, by Christopher Tunnard, the period's leading proponent of a modern theory of landscape and garden design. Landscape, architecture and sculpture each operated here by carving into form to uncover a concealed reality. Such activity illustrates the theory developed by Adrian Stokes in his book *Colour and Form* in 1937 from his earlier writings on Italian Renaissance low-relief sculpture. Stokes, a dedicated admirer of Nicholson and Hepworth who nonetheless chose The Euston Road School when beginning his career as a painter, had recently completed a period of psychoanalysis with Melanie Klein, a pupil of Freud, who explored the enduring effects of conflicting states of infantile fantasy and their role in structuring experience. 'Carving creates a face for the stone, as agriculture for the earth, as man for woman,' wrote Stokes. 'Modelling is a more purely plastic creation, it does not disclose, as a face, the significance of what already exists.'[30] Here, more convincingly, perhaps, than Piper was ever able to demonstrate in his painting, was the answer to his challenge about the tree in the field, of restoring technique as a process of research. Richard Wolheim comments on the way that 'the adoption of the new concepts helped to free Stokes's theory from any residual chronological reference'.[31] As with Grigson's pronouncement on the irrelevance of historical time, the refusal of an evolutionary concept of Modernism, necessarily and continuously differentiated from what had gone before, became the true liberation from the past. Stokes also borrowed the concept of 'identity in difference' from the philosopher F H Bradley to describe the reality lying behind simple categories, seen in painting in the phenomenon of simultaneous contrast.

Rather than art being a question of abstract good, everything else bad, as Nicholson had tended to insist from 1935 onwards, Stokes offered a choice based on the science of the mind rather than the science of abstract form. For Coldstream, this was a decisive point. 'His [Stokes's] influence was to make me feel that the thing really was to do what one wanted to do, even if one was not enormously equipped to do it, rather than to follow out theories of what one ought to do.'[32]

Many commentators have regretted the loss of a cutting edge in English Modernism in the period immediately before the war, but the shift was significant not as a replacement of one totalising system by another but, at best, as a rejection of all such systems as destructive of humanity. The hope that design would reveal a deeper level of truth through form, which seemed so important at the beginning of the decade, changed to a more interactive relationship with the immediate world. The 'All Europe House' presented by the housing reformer Elizabeth Denby at the Ideal Home Exhibition in 1939 and entirely furnished by women, was a two-storey terrace, a

[30] Adrian Stokes, *Colour and Form*, London, 1937, p.41.

[31] Richard Wolheim, introduction to *The Image in Form: selected writings of Adrian Stokes*, Harmondsworth, 1972, p.20.

[32] Quoted in Lawrence Gowing, 'Remembering Coldstream' in *The Paintings of William Coldstream 1908–87*, London, 1990.

[33] Paul Greenhalgh, 'The English Compromise: modern design and national consciousness 1870–1940', in Wendy Kaplan (ed.), *Designing Modernity*, London, 1995.

[34] Louis MacNeice, *Autumn Journal*, London, 1939, p.95.

realisation, to borrow Stokes's phrase, of 'the significance of what already exists', a prototype for an architecture of social realism and an implied criticism of architects who were yearning to build cities of high-rise flats.

If the abandonment of the grand designs of Modernism was a 'structured compromise' as Paul Greenhalgh describes it,[33] it was not gained without difficulty and moral courage in the face of many pressures to prefer universal solutions. In terms of the proposition advanced at the outset, this deliberate choice of a critical position was representative of a deeper meaning of Modernism which chooses the messy reality of life instead of manic orderliness. Only in this way can Modernism be represented as a continuing movement rather than as a historically-specific style. It did not involve a retreat into the past or into ruralism, but, in a time of dreams and nightmares, a more realistic restatement of the political role of art and design, dealing with actual people rather than abstractions. The position which a number of artists and thinkers had reached at the end of the decade, when another war was only a matter of time, was put by Louis MacNeice in *Autumn Journal*, published in May 1939:

Chair by Berthold Lubetkin for his own apartment, The Penthouse, Highpoint II, Highgate. Courtesy of Penthouse, Highpoint. Photo: John Riddy.

. . . shall our dream be earnest of the real
Future when we wake,
Design a home, a factory, a fortress
Which, though with effort, we can really make?
What is it we want really?
For what end and how?
If it is something feasible, obtainable,
Let us dream it now,
And pray for a possible land
Not of sleep-walkers and angry puppets,
But where both heart and brain can understand
The movements of our fellows;
Where life is a choice of instruments and none
Is debarred his natural music,
Where the waters of life are free of the ice-blockade of hunger
And thought is free as the sun,
Where the altars of sheer power and mere profit
Have fallen to disuse,
Where nobody sees the use
Of buying money and blood at the cost of blood and money,
Where the individual, no longer squandered
In self-assertion, works with the rest, endowed
With the split vision of a juggler and the quick lock of a taxi,
Where the people are more than a crowd.[34]

Lubetkin and Tecton, Penguin Pool,
Regent's Park Zoo, under construction, 1934.
Photograph: British Architectural Library,
RIBA, London.

In Search of Modernity: The Urban Projects of the Modern Movement, 1929–39

JOHN R GOLD

'The *British* Modern Movement?' said the elderly professor interviewing a prospective doctoral student in the mid-1970s, 'In the *interwar* period? I never knew there was one.' It was then a common sentiment. Few architectural historians attached much importance to the small number of British-based architects who allied themselves to the international Modern Movement in the interwar years. The prevailing view was that architectural Modernism only became an effective force once it permeated the curricula of the architectural schools in the 1950s and offered recipes that seemed to meet the needs of postwar urban reconstruction. Before that time, the overwhelming conservatism of British architects apparently held it in check.

Subsequent reappraisal has softened these assertions. In the first place, British architecture was not universally conservative. The legacy of architects such as Voysey, Charles Rennie Mackintosh, Webb and Lethaby attracted those concerned about the orientation of contemporary architecture. The Garden City movement acted as a natural home for progressive exercises in housing or city design, with strong relationships between the social architecture of that movement and the theory and practice of "new architecture" favoured by modernists.

Secondly, a recognisable Modern Movement had appeared before the Second World War, even if it lacked the high profile of kindred movements in Continental Europe. A loosely-associated group of modern architects had emerged, principally in the London area.[1] By 1939 they had appropriated the mantle of the architectural avant-garde, built up valuable connections with the media, and consolidated an infrastructure of pressure groups, short-lived periodicals, exhibitions and informal meeting places. Their views on most issues concerned with design and the political orientation of architecture varied enormously, but there was a powerful dynamic towards finding common ground. As one close observer noted:

Like all these movements, it included people with different approaches, which appear to be the same in the early days. Before the war, the differences were concealed because of the fact that the revolution had barely taken off – it was still nascent – and therefore the emphasis was on a common approach.[2]

Areas in which beliefs and orientations converged were therefore assiduously cultivated. These included preferences for unornamented exteriors for buildings, advanced constructional techniques, new building materials (eg. steel, glass and reinforced concrete), and use of new energy sources, especially electricity. The spirit of the times was considered tied to the development of scientific ration-ality. At one level, this promoted interest in the potential of mecha-nisation and standardisation for industrialised building production. At another level, it underpinned a growing belief in the need for architects 'as creative artists . . . [to be] concerned with a future which must be planned'.[3]

'Planning' was a term with distinct resonances. For a minority on the Left, it carried connotations of the systems of planning found in the Soviet Union, where architecture took its place alongside other design professions as a force for social transformation. For others, the debate centred specifically on *town planning* and the possibility of expanding the architect's sphere of influence. Traditionally, professional architecture in Britain was associated with specially-commissioned buildings for commercial, civic, ecclesiastical or wealthy private clients. The needs of modern life, it was argued, now supported the logic of coordinating and integrating design at all spatial scales. What was wanted was for:

. . . architecture to have its chance. The only way that it could be appreciated to the full was if there was a rational base on which it could be constructed, namely logical design with form following function at all levels from the chair to the region and, if possible, extending even further.[4]

There were, of course, tactical advantages for architects in staking out a position that might secure themselves a share in the work forthcoming whenever comprehensive planning systems were adopted. Nevertheless, there was a consensus supporting the notion of planning as a social ideal, motivated particularly by wishing to improve the quality of life in the industrial cities of Britain.

By any standard, those cities were in crisis. City centres suffered from severe land shortage and traffic congestion (Figure 1). Working-class districts close to the core were overcrowded and decrepit; conditions that had already prompted the national slum clearance campaign. Beyond the core, especially along the major rail lines and arterial roads, lay suburban estates speculatively built by private

Notes

[1] For biographical detail on the mixture of British- and overseas-trained architects who comprised this group, see John R Gold, *The Experience of Modernism: modern architects and the future city, 1928–53*, London, 1997, pp.88–93.

[2] Statement by Percy Johnson-Marshall, interview with J R Gold, 9 December 1986.

[3] Quoted in D Dean, *The Thirties: recalling the English architectural scene*, London, 1983, p.22.

[4] Statement by Arthur Ling, interview with J R Gold, 20 January 1987.

Figure 1
Traffic Congestion in Regent's Street,
London, 1932.
Photograph: CAM Collection,
Frances Loeb Library, Harvard University.

5 N Evenson, *Le Corbusier: the machine and the grand design*, London, 1969, p.9.

6 With regard to the early town planning work of CIAM see E Mumford, 'CIAM urbanism after the Athens Charter', *Planning Perspectives*, 7,1992, pp.391–417 and John R Gold, 'Creating the Charter of Athens: CIAM and the Functional City, 1933–43', *Town Planning Review*, 69, 1998, pp. 221–43. It should also be stressed that, although commonly treated as virtually synonymous with early twentieth-century European Modernism, 'functionalism' has older roots and far wider cultural references. For further discussion, see E R De Zurko, *Origins of Functionalist Theory*, New York, 1957.

7 Interview with Lord Esher, 15 April 1987.

8 Particularly the London-based Architectural Press, which actively propagated the cause of architectural Modernism after 1930 through its monographs and periodicals.

9 For example, an official delegation from Birmingham toured Germany, Austria and Czechoslovakia in 1930, with the London County Council sending delegations to Germany, Austria, Czechoslovakia, Holland, France and Scandinavia in 1935.

10 Such work was poorly paid and had relatively low status.

developers. The London conurbation had doubled in area since 1919, devouring the countryside and causing alarm about the accretion of seemingly formless suburbs at the urban fringe. Urban transport systems were antiquated and suffered from under-investment.

Against this background, modern architects argued that the challenge of planning required finding 'a new and comprehensively ordered urban ambient'[5] that fully expressed *modernity* – the quality or condition of being modern. The favoured approach drew on a functional analysis that was initially proposed in 1928 at the first congress of Les Congrès Internationaux d'Architecture Moderne (CIAM), the international forum for modern architecture.[6] This analysis identified three key elements of the city – dwelling, work and leisure – connected by a fourth: circulation (transport and communications). The key to building cities that functioned efficiently and harmoniously was to identify the requirements of each of these elements and to avoid conflicts between them.

This essay examines some attempts by British modern architects to explore the relationships between the 'new architecture' and urban forms. The next section deals with British architects' involvement in experimental designs for housing schemes that went beyond mere supply of dwelling spaces to embrace frameworks for 'modern life'. The subsequent sections explore the realm of imagination, examining unrealised projects that articulated, through drawings and three-dimensional models, the spatial language of the prospective city.

Social Housing

Housing occupied a prime place in the priorities of the early Modern Movement; indeed many would have subscribed to the view that 'it was through housing that we saw cities being rebuilt'.[7] From 1930 onwards, sympathetic sections of the architectural press[8] and official visits from British civic delegations[9] helped spread awareness in Britain of the innovative estates of worker housing being created in the Netherlands, Belgium, Austria and Weimar Germany. These estates gave modern architects the chance to put unfamiliar ideas about the design, construction and layout of built forms to the general public. They showed how housing people in blocks of flats could coordinate provision of dwelling space with provision of services and open space. Above all, they hinted at how architecture could be used to promote new communal ways of life.

In the short-term, opportunities to emulate their continental counterparts proved difficult to achieve. Many residential buildings with overtly modernist exteriors were primarily essays in style. Private developers in South-coast seaside resorts like Brighton and St Leonards, for example, consciously appropriated Le Corbusier's analogy of the decks of an ocean liner to devise an imagery apposite to the marine environment (Figure 2). Few modern architects worked or even sought work in the public sector.[10] Experimentation with newer forms of flatted estates, therefore, usually depended on the interests of the chief architect or engineer of individual munici-

Figure 2
Marine Court, St Leonards on Sea, 1935–7.
Photograph: author's collection.

43

palities. In Liverpool, for example, Lancelot Keay adopted the aesthetics and elements of layout from the public housing schemes of pre-1934 Socialist Vienna (Figure 3). At the Quarry Hill estate in Leeds (1933), R A H Livett had combined modernistic styling with the Mopin industrialised building system devised in France.

Figure 3
L H Keay, Gerard Gardens, Liverpool, 1936.
Photograph: British Architectural Library, RIBA, London.

Conscious applications of modernist principles in an attempt to reshape patterns of life were rare and tended to be sponsored by wealthy private patrons. Wells Coates's Lawn Road development in Hampstead (1932–4), for instance, provided an experiment with much smaller-scale flats than normally found in such schemes.[11] The rationale lay in the quality of service provision. When completed, the rents included bed-making, shoe-cleaning, laundry and window-cleaning services, with the availability of hot meals from the staff canteen. The rationale, according to Coates, was that 'new habits of life' demanded a response from architects:

We don't possess our homes in the old, permanent, settled sense; we move from place to place, to find work or to find new surroundings . . . We don't want to spend as much as we used to on our homes. So the first thing is that our dwellings have got to be much smaller than they used to be . . . we cannot burden ourselves with permanent tangible possessions, as well as our real new possessions of freedom, travel, new experience – in short, what we call life.[12]

Nevertheless, Lawn Road's combination of high rents and aura of social experimentation meant that the new residents were primarily recruited from 'enlightened' members of the upper-middle class. A similar outcome resulted from another seminal development, Lubetkin and Tecton's Highpoint I and II (Figures 4 and 5), built between 1933 and 1938. Highpoint I quickly became luxury flats leavened with a few units let at low rents, even though the project started life as a scheme for workers' housing for Zigmund Gestetner, the office machinery manufacturer.[13]

Kensal House (Ladbroke Grove, London, 1936–7) was an exception to the rule that experiments in progressive housing soon became

[11] Coates was influenced by personal experience of Japanese dwellings and by the idea of the *Existenzminimum* ('Minimum habitation') devised by Ernst May's social housing in Frankfurt. May and his colleagues maximised the number of dwelling units created by means of such devices as extensive use of ingenious built-in storage, foldaway beds and kitchen design. Notably, Coates's client at Lawn Road was the furniture manufacturer Jack Pritchard.

[12] W W Coates, 'Modern Dwellings for Modern Needs' (conversation with G Boumphrey), *The Listener*, 24 May 1933.

[13] It was to have been built at a site in Camden Town.

filled with the local avant-garde. Designed by Maxwell Fry, with a committee that included Robert Atkinson, C H James, G Grey Wornum and the housing reformer Elizabeth Denby, Kensal House offered a wide range of social and communal facilities besides providing housing for the working class. The estate incorporated a community centre, kindergarten, crèche, communal laundry and canteen facilities. Residents were also represented on committees and other bodies involved in the estate's management. Overall the scheme was presented as offering a progressive and comprehensive approach to planning, and a modest prototype for modern living.

Imagined Cities
Student Projects

The changing climate of ideas within the architectural profession started to influence the curriculum of the architectural schools after 1935. Perhaps the most innovative work came from the Architectural Association, where changes in teaching structures encouraged students to undertake lengthy project work. Two such projects that stand out are the Ocean Street Study (1939) and 'Tomorrow Town' (1937–8).

The former broke new ground by pioneering techniques of public participation in planning. Ocean Street (Stepney) was a 'clearance

Figure 4
Lubetkin and Tecton.
An aerial view of Highpoint I, 1933–35.
'Modern Flats in Highgate',
Architectural Review, 84, p.161.

Figure 5
Lubetkin and Tecton. One of the two-storey
living rooms in the duplex flats in Highpoint II
'Modern Flats in Highgate',
Architectural Review, 84, p. 168

area' where the London County Council (LCC) aimed to demolish 729 houses designated as 'slums' and replace them with 15 five-storey blocks of flats. Finding little correlation between the residents' preferences for 'houses' and the flats proposed by the LCC, the students formulated alternative plans. Working within the financial and legal constraints of the clearance legislation, they produced a scheme that combined duplex-units of two-storey flats into a low-rise flatted estate. The 'houses' in this arrangement therefore qualified as flats for funding. The existing conditions were photographed, a model of the proposals was made, and a scripted film made of the residents' case.[14]

'Tomorrow Town' (Figure 6) was a study for a new town of 50,000 people carried out in 1937–8 by students under the direction of E A A Rowse. The scheme was originally produced as a rectilinear plan for a hypothetical flat site, but was subsequently applied to a site at Farringdon (Oxfordshire). The new town comprised five neighbourhood units,[15] each housing 2,000 families, located around the town centre. The dwellings, which would be factory-produced and assembled on-site, comprised both flats and terraced houses. Twelve-storey flats were placed to the east and west of a town centre set in a park. Further to the east and west were lower density areas of terraced housing that also contained the necessary social services for the community living there. A green belt separated the town from its industrial areas to the north and east, with the latter, being downwind, housing any noxious industries. The town centre contained the rail and bus stations. Perimeter roads surrounding the residential areas and town centres catered for motorised transport, with entirely separate circulation systems for pedestrians and cyclists.[16]

Planning For London

Students were not the only ones mapping out potential urban futures. From 1933 onwards, members of the London-based Modern Architectural Research (MARS) Group worked on projects that eventually led to the publication of their *Master Plan for London* in July 1942.[17] While the date of publication of this document places it outside the scope of this essay, two preliminary studies indicate both the trend and plurality of thought about city design.

The first was the work of William and Aileen Tatton Brown, in collaboration with the publisher Hubert de Cronin Hastings. First presented to the Fifth Congress of CIAM in Paris (September 1937),[18] the plan primarily comprised ideas for handling urban growth stimulated by projected rises in car ownership. Its conceptual basis was a 'Theory of Contacts', which asserted that the city's prime function

[14] Max Lock Centre Exhibition Research Group, *Max Lock, 1909–88: People and Planning, an Exhibition of his Life and Work*, London, 1997. The scheme received considerable publicity with press briefings and public meetings, but had achieved little official support before the outbreak of war put an end to further discussions.

[15] The concept of the 'neighbourhood unit' was derived from the work of Clarence Perry on the First Regional Plan of New York. They were essentially housing estates for 5,000–10,000 people built with integral social services: indeed the size was often predicated on the rule that no child should need to walk more than a half-mile to school. They had excited interest on both sides of the Atlantic as possible building blocks for the construction of new settlements.

[16] P L Cocke, 'Tomorrow Town', in J Gowan (ed.) *Projects: Architectural Association, 1946–71*, London, 1973, and M Pattrick, 'Architectural aspirations', *AA Journal*, January 1958, pp.153–4.

[17] A Korn and F J Samuely, 'A Master Plan for London', *Architectural Review*, 91, 1942, pp. 143–50.

[18] CIAM, *Logis et Loisirs*, Paris, 1937.

was to maximise opportunities for human contacts (or transactions), whether intellectual, social or commercial. Efficient communications were essential in achieving that goal and this, in turn, required recognition of the different speeds of traffic. Four categories were proposed: pedestrian movement (below 10 km/hr), local traffic (up to 100 km/hr), rapid highway traffic (more than 100 km/hr), and air travel. Traffic systems were devised accordingly.

The plan envisaged channelling London's growth between 1935 and 1950 into 13 linear strips that radiated into the surrounding countryside. Each was centred on a high-speed, high-density through-road, seeking to convert the dynamic that caused unplanned ribbon development into the precursors of a new urban form. Residential developments would be sited parallel to the spinal roads, but screened from them by earthworks and the roads' sunken level. Multi-level intersections at one-mile intervals provided access for traffic destined for, or joining from, the 'neighbourhood units'.

Figure 7 shows the hypothetical layout of a one-mile long neighbourhood unit designed to supply homes, amenities and a substantial part of the employment for a population of 3,340. Housing was differentiated by the socio-economic status of householders into 'producers' (working class), 'distributors' (middle class) and 'consumers' (upper class). Residential accommodation comprised 480 flats and 380 conventional houses. As seen in Figure 7, the houses

Figure 6
Service road with terrace housing (upper) and houses merging into flats (lower), 'Tomorrow Town' (4th and 5th Year Town Planning and Housing Group, Architectural Association), 1937–8.
J Gowan (ed.), *Projects: Architectural Association, 1946–71*, London: Architectural Association, p.8.

situated on the sinuous distribution road consisted of both villas and modern terraced housing, with an average density of five dwellings per acre. The flats, by contrast, were clustered around the neighbourhood centre. They comprised eight multi-storey blocks, each of 60 flats, with a double-cruciform plan reminiscent of the design for Highpoint I (see Figure 4). The individual neighbourhood units, in turn, combined into linear strips. Figure 8 shows how ten units might be assembled to provide homes and employment for approximately 30,000 people. Protection of the green spaces between the strips of development would ensure that residents had easy access to nearby open space and fresh air.

Although regarded as innovative, the mixture of flatted accommodation and conventional housing and the assumption of continuing social differentiation did not appeal to many other members of the MARS Group. A subsequent plan, prepared by Arthur Ling in 1938, proposed an alternative arrangement of residential accommodation based purely in blocks of flats.[19] These made reference to two aspects of Continental European practice. First, the layout of the blocks of flats replicated the German *Zeilenbau* pattern of north-south alignment, with windows facing east and west to afford the maximum light. Secondly, the blocks themselves were influenced by Le Corbusier's concept of the *unité d'habitation* in which flats and social facilities were combined in a single domestic structure.

The residential areas were arranged hierarchically into five levels. These comprised: residential units of 1,000 people, neighbourhood units (6,000), town or borough units (50,000), city or regional units (500,000) and the capital city (5 million). The first two levels in this scheme are shown in Figure 9. The residential units fitted together in a cellular structure arranged around a central corridor, in which were the educational and community services for the neighbourhood. Traffic within the residential units would be solely for access; traffic within the neighbourhood units purely local. Through traffic was kept to the outside margins. Four such blocks were laid out to the north and four to the south of a corridor (Figure 10) that contained civic amenities, sports facilities and parkland, to comprise a borough unit. This would be bounded north and south by through-roads from which distribution arteries would connect at regular intervals. Ten borough units might then combine into the city units, with the city itself comprising ten city units.

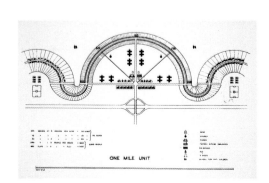

Figure 7
One Mile Unit (neighbourhood unit)
Personal Papers, W E Tatton Brown.

The Concrete City

Three-dimensional models also played a part in popularising ideas about the urban future. The 'Concrete City' designed by F R S Yorke and Marcel Breuer, for example, explored principles for central city

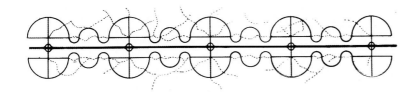

FIVE   ONE   MILE   UNITS   POPULATION   30,000

Figure 8
An example of a Linear Strip formed from an aggregation of neighbourhood units.
Personal papers, W E Tatton Brown.

redevelopment. This was built at 1:360 scale for the Cement and Concrete Association in 1936. Measuring 290 x 170 cm (Figure 11) and originally entitled 'A Garden City of the Future', the 'Concrete City' regularly appeared at various design and architectural exhibitions between 1936 to 1938.[20]

Its aim was to serve as a 'demonstration of principle' and was a pastiche intended to cram as many different features as possible into a small space. It only showed a portion of the central area of a city bordering on to a lake, but this was considered large enough to show the relationship between land-uses as well as appropriate transport systems. From this basis, its designers sought to show the interrelationship of residential, retail, commercial, industrial and recreational land-uses as well as appropriate transport systems to a public unfamiliar with such ideas.

It embraced three design principles: geometrically-regular layout, strict functional separation of land-uses, and segregation of traffic flows. The housing again made reference to the *Zeilenbau* pattern and the *unité d'habitation*, with shops placed at the ends of blocks and schools centrally grouped between the blocks. It was stressed that the model only showed part of the city and that lower-rise flats and even individual houses would be built near the fringe. To some extent, however, the decisions on housing reflected the policy on movement within the city. As Yorke and Breuer noted:

the adoption of higher buildings ensures . . . the distances from point to point are reduced to a minimum. With this type of plan too, the simplification of traffic conditions becomes automatic, there are fewer house doors, fewer streets, and above all, fewer street intersections. [. . .] The private house in the centre of the city complicates immediately the traffic problem.[21]

Transport flows would be channelled into purpose-built, high-capacity routeways of the type exemplified by the axial road that ran across the model. Through-traffic could move unimpeded; traffic serving the megastructural retailing district, the water-front entertainment district or the office complexes, could leave

[19] This scheme was based on a thesis that he had recently completed: A G Ling, 'Social Units', unpublished Diploma thesis, Department of Town and Country Planning, University College, University of London, 1938. Ling stressed that his thesis looked towards having a mix of flats and conventional houses-with-gardens, but agreed to prepare a new version based on flats at the request of Arthur Korn, Chairman of the MARS Group's Town Planning Committee.

[20] These included the 1936 Ideal Home Exhibition and the MARS Group's 1938 'New Architecture' exhibition.

[21] F R S Yorke and M Breuer, 'A Garden City of the Future', in J L Martin, B Nicholson and N Gabo (eds.), *Circle: International Survey of Constructive Art*, London, 1937, pp.182–3.

or join the axial road by a modified clover-leaf intersection. Parking spaces or other indications of where vehicles were to be left when not in use are virtually absent from this conception.

Conclusion

Visions of housing and schools in green spaces, geometric harmony and superhighways, fine architecture and communal societies: all the ingredients of the utopia-turned-dystopia that popular opinion now associates with Modernism. Yet care must be taken when revisiting the plans, models and housing

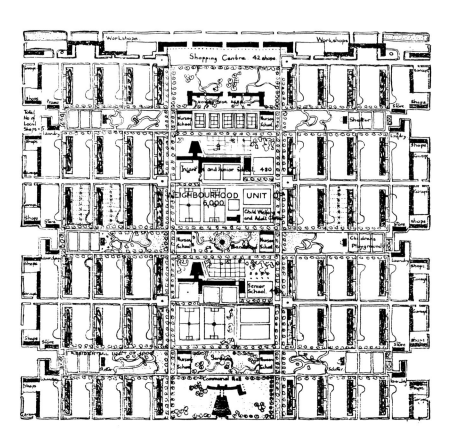

Figure 9
An example of a neighbourhood unit.
Personal papers, Professor A G Ling.

projects produced by the British Modern Movement in the 1930s. Quite simply, in these early days positions on design matters were fluid and ideologies were malleable. In seeking to create propaganda for the new scope and vision of modern architecture, modern architects gave expression to their beliefs in the methods of the scientist, the engineer, and the industrialist, in the functional arrangement of cities, and in the logical imperative of planning. Belief in planning drew them towards hazy conceptions of a new society that could be realised by enlightened architecture.

Yet paper is cheap. It was not obligatory to think through every detail before picking up the drafting pen. Nor did architects, as

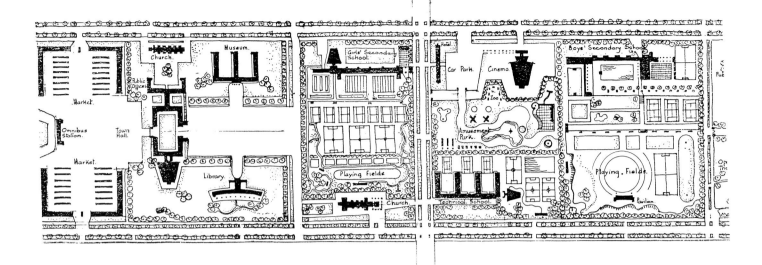

Figure 10
Part of the central corridor of a borough unit,
showing parkland and civic facilities.
Personal papers, Professor A G Ling.

people on the fringes of their profession with little immediate
prospect of building anything substantial, feel it necessary to scruti-
nise every word before writing manifestos. Simplistic slogans were
meant as a way of getting a point across rather than as fuel for mem-
oirs or historians. To look back on this period is to detect the hopes
of a movement striving for an architecture that captured the spirit of
modernity long before the lessons of experience could under-mine
the cheerful idealism of their initial visions. Scrutiny of the historical
record reveals plurality and experimentation, not over-arching
blueprints for the future city or of its society. At a time when
criticisms of architectural Modernism's vision and contribution at
the city-scale have become so routinely negative and stereotyped,
these points are valuable counterweights to prevailing orthodoxy.

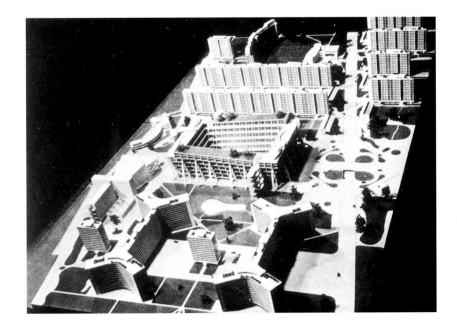

Figure 11
F R S Yorke and Marcel Breuer, The Concrete
City, 1936. 'A Garden City of the Future', in
J L Martin, B Nicholson and N Gabo (eds.),
Circle, London, p.183.

A Living Tradition:
Modernism and the Decorative Arts

JANE FRASER AND LIZ PAUL

Industrial Art Collection,
Manchester City Art Gallery, 1939.

Some of the very best pieces of English art are produced by trades with a strong and live tradition . . . All this is distinctively conservative, it is not exciting, but it shows a dignity and balance possible only in a country whose traditions have never been blocked by any revolution. The typical English attitude towards tradition and modernity may be illustrated by two quotations. The first is taken from Lethaby's writings: 'We ought to recognize tradition and add something which shall be the tradition of the future.' In accordance with this, Mr Frank Pick once said that industrial design in this country should be 'modest and not grandiose in scale . . . not too logical in form . . . a reasonable compromise between beauty and utility, neither overstressing beauty till it degenerates into ornament, nor overstressing utility until it becomes bare and hard'.[1]

In 1929, when design reformers believed that Britain was on the threshold of making a significant contribution to the Modern Movement, Lawrence Haward, Curator of Manchester City Art Gallery, started to collect contemporary decorative art. The Industrial Art Collection, as it was to be known, was developed over a period of ten years and comprised ceramics, glass, textiles and commercial printing.[2] Haward, a founder member of the Manchester branch of the Design and Industries Association and a committed supporter of art and design education, outlined his philosophy in 1921: 'For it is little use to ask the average man (or indeed anyone else) to keep his mind sensitive to the beauty of ancient Greece or Italy if we do nothing to help him have good well-designed things around him in his private life. Art like charity, begins at home.'[3]

Haward was responding to a tradition of art and design education in Manchester. The Industrial Art Collection was aimed primarily at the consumer – manufacturer, retailer, and middleman were all ultimately consumers, but the education of the shopping public was Haward's main intention. Although, in retrospect, the collection

Notes

[1] Nikolaus Pevsner, *An Enquiry into Industrial Art in England*, Cambridge, 1937, pp.285–6.

[2] See Jane Fraser and Liz Paul, 'Art, Industry and Everyday Things – Manchester City Art Galleries and Industrial Art between the Wars', *Journal of the Decorative Art Society*, 1998, for a full discussion of Manchester's Industrial Art Collection.

[3] Lawrence Haward, 'The Function of Art Museums', *Museums Journal*, 21, December 1921, p.121.

included few affordable, mass-produced everyday objects, and reveals more about the attitude of the intellectual middle classes to design reform, a sense of responsibility provided its foundation. Instead of lamenting the state of British design, and taking refuge in Manchester's historic collections, Haward sought out the best design of the period and encouraged visitors to the gallery to do likewise. Manufacturers varied from the unhelpful to the very supportive. A E Gray, of Gray's Pottery, was a consistent and generous donor to the collection, as was Captain Turnbull of the cotton printing firm, Turnbull and Stockdale, one of only three contributors amongst the Manchester-based textile firms.

Stylistically, the Industrial Art Collection encompassed the many different strands of 1930s' modern taste, from a muted 'jazz modern', through architecturalism and, towards the end of the decade, a revived classicism. Within it foreign influences interacted with native styles – the French inspired angularities of Art Deco and the balanced grace of Swedish design were juxtaposed with the legacy of the Arts and Crafts Movement. Whilst the Industrial Art Collection was broadly Modernist in conception, it was both traditional and nationalist in scope – a decorative art collection, limited by the historical precedent of the gallery's existing collections, and the expectations of the governors. The term *industrial art* was essentially defined by mass production in a factory or workshop environment. But traditional craft-based industries predominated, industries that were usually only semi-mechanised, and if mass production excluded artist craftsmen, it could include workshop producers. Tradition, although unaccredited by Haward, lay at the root of the Manchester collection.

Tradition was a word often used by design writers but rarely defined. Broadly speaking, it combined an awareness of British history and historical styles with a sensitivity to what was perceived to be the national character. During the 1930s, writers sought an interpretation of British tradition that was neither limiting nor xenophobic, and which combined the rationality of the eighteenth century with a less easily identified unconscious tradition, a form of 'race genius'. Within this tradition was a recognition of the enduring nature of classic forms, a respect for the pioneering work of William Morris, and an appreciation of British engineering and craftsmanship of the nineteenth century. This characterised an intellectually aware and practical interpretation of tradition; a tradition that would enrich rather than reject Modernism, and create an enduring and distinctively British identity by absorbing and reinterpreting Modernism within terms of the national consciousness. The ideal was a Modernist way of life, fully integrated within the British tradition, that went beyond style mongering and would foster national self-confidence whilst creating a highly exportable and saleable image abroad.

ART AMONG THE CROCKS

EV. NEWS · 9.10.33

Even the rolling pin can now be made to brighten up the kitchen as this young woman found at the Industrial Art Exhibition, which opened at Manchester Art Gallery to-day

Manchester Evening News, 9 October 1933. As well as acquiring contemporary design for the permanent collection, the City Art Gallery also hosted several touring exhibitions during the decade, including the influential 'British Industrial Art in Relation to the Home' in October 1933, first shown at Dorland Hall earlier that year. The local press responded positively, encouraging young housewives in particular to visit the gallery.

Royal Lancastrian Pottery made by Pilkington's Tile and Pottery Company, and Monart Glass by John Moncrieff Ltd, acquired from the British Industries Fair in 1930. The first acquisitions were made for the Industrial Art Collection; these pieces illustrate its basis in traditional, semi-mechanised industries that still relied heavily on handmaking processes.

According to critic John Gloag, the lost golden age of design was believed to be between about 1670 and 1820, when 'things as different as coaches, barges, chairs, lamps and door-knockers were shaped and embellished in a manner that made them members of one large, gracious family whose outstanding characteristic was elegant proportion. An architecturally-educated public then existed. It does not today.'[4]

The admiration for the eighteenth century, with its unity of production and design, and coherent society, seems to have been universal, although writers were quick to point out that differing social conditions made it an impractical model. But if it could not be directly imitated, there was much that could be taken from the eighteenth-century approach to life. Paul Nash, writing in the *Architectural Review* in 1930, explained the lesson of Robert Adam:

Robert Adam had vision . . . The fact that this vision was not entirely original, that the Adam style was based upon Renaissance, Roman, Greek and French work, detracts in no way from its significance; rather it emphasizes the peculiar genius of the Brothers for extracting from foreign material an essence with which they founded a style not only personal but national . . . We are faced today with much the same task as that which the Brothers undertook in the early part of the eighteenth century. We are invaded by very strong influences; we possess certain solid traditions.[5]

The popularity of Adam probably contributed to the encouragement of architects to take the lead as designers. In the absence of a feudal society – credited for the eighteenth-century achievement with its rule of taste imposed from above – there was strong support for the idea of a responsible genius with collective ideals. Josiah Wedgwood was another 'cult' figure, especially as a model for the pottery industry, and admiringly-captioned illustrations of eighteenth-century Wedgwood were ubiquitous well into the 1950s. Herbert Read wrote, in 1934, of Wedgwood:

4 John Gloag, 'Men and Buildings', quoted by P Morton Shand in 'Reveille', *Architectural Review*, September 1931, p.75.

5 Paul Nash, 'Modern English Furnishing', *Architectural Review*, January 1930, pp.43–4.

6 Herbert Read, *Art and Industry*, London, 1934, pp.26–7.

7 Royal Academy, *British Industrial Art*, London, 1935, p.11.

His useful wares, in which his true genius was expressed, are still with us, for we can hardly eat from a plate or drink from a cup that does not bear the impress of his practical genius . . . The useful wares which have survived were the product of the local pottery tradition, selected and refined by the practical genius of Wedgwood, himself a trained potter. In English Pottery, *a book written by Mr Bernard Rackham and myself ten years ago, we observed of these useful wares that 'Wedgwood was the first potter to think out forms which should be thoroughly well suited to their purpose, and at the same time capable of duplication with precision in unlimited quantities . . .' In these words we defined a machine art in its first phase, and with all its essential features.*[6]

Thus Wedgwood was an exemplar who drew upon, rather than rejected, the existing craft tradition; created practical styles and shapes of such excellence that they were still in production; and, through his business acumen, shared the genius of his creative yet orderly mind. The Wedgwood factory exploited Josiah Wedgwood's legacy, using the slogan 'A Living Tradition' to advertise both reproduction and modern wares, and during the early 1930s consciously positioned itself as design leader of the pottery industry. As Josiah Wedgwood had made earthenware fashionable in the eighteenth century, with its connotations of democracy and utility, so Wedgwood kept its own earthenware at the forefront of contemporary design, through its own design studios and by employing outside designers, such as Keith Murray. Trained as an architect, Murray worked freelance in ceramics, glass and metalwork, and purely in design terms perhaps comes closest to the ideal of a responsible genius. Haward, a consistent consumer of approved taste, purchased Murray-designed ceramics and glass for the Industrial Art Collection throughout the 1930s. In these pieces, Murray's style can be seen developing from an architectural Modernism with its roots in Swedish design into a pared-down, eighteenth-century classicism.

While, superficially, cleaner eighteenth-century designs accorded well with modern taste, ideas of order and rationality, both associated with the eighteenth century, were examples of shared virtues that could be usefully applied to any age. In the early 1930s this philosophy manifested itself in an emphasis on form, line and plain, undecorated surfaces. In Haward's Industrial Art Collection, Carter, Stabler and Adam's (Poole) 'Picotee' tea wares of 1933, and a Gray's Pottery lustre tea set illustrated in the Royal Academy's 'British Art in Industry' exhibition catalogue, have clear eighteenth-century antecedents.[7] By the late 1930s the Georgian revival was fully underway. Haward purchased Ramsden Wood Print Works glazed chintzes printed with cherubs and urns from the Royal Institute of British Architects' *Exhibition of Everyday Things* in 1936, and in 1939 an urn-shaped vase designed by Keith Murray for the glass firm of Stevens and Williams.

Advertisement for Wedgwood's Annular tableware, *Pottery Gazette & Glass Trade Review*, June 1933.

Tracing themes of order and rationality through the nineteenth century proved somewhat harder. However, Harold Curwen related the century's engineering achievements to contemporary printing when he stated both literally and metaphorically: 'In judging printed matter, there are, as with engineering, gauges and standards which can be brought into use for comparison.'[8] This statement encompassed much of the printing in the Industrial Art Collection, from the tidy presentation of Empire Marketing Board and London Passenger Transport Board posters, the uncluttered typefaces of Monotype, to the clear layouts of Curwen's own firm, the Curwen Press. Equally, the rehabilitation of lithographic printing on ceramics, in particular Wedgwood earthenwares with transfer-printed designs by Eric Ravilious (drawing consciously on eighteenth-century black-printed creamwares), rationalised ceramic decoration. Hand-painted decoration in the industrial context was attractive and popular with the consumer, but was no more than a cipher for creative means of expression.

The achievements of the eighteenth century were easily identifiable, and a comforting reminder of past glories. More elusive was the concept of 'unconscious tradition' which manifested itself both in social and aesthetic virtues. Its social virtues were largely beyond the scope of Manchester's Industrial Art Collection. Haward was not a collector of the beleaguered rural crafts, with their unity of design and

Earthenware bowl designed by Keith Murray for Wedgwood, acquired for the Industrial Art Collection from the British Industrial Art Exhibition of 1933.

production, which were of peripheral relevance to the citizens of Manchester. The 'unconscious tradition' was by implication continuous, fundamental rather than developmental, and to a certain extent instinctive and expressive. In an uncorrupted time-scale, parallel to the chaos induced by the machine age, the British tradition survived, and in the best cases adapted itself to the modern world. Pevsner cited several such examples in 1937, particularly in the long-established textile and pottery industries:

It now remains to seek for reasons that might explain the exemplary quality of some, and the creditable qualities of most, British furnishing materials . . . Of prime importance no doubt is the strong and indigenous tradition in prints as well as in weaves. English prints have flourished ever since the days of the Tudors and right down to the time of Morris and his followers; and British woven tweeds, etc., of perfect design and workmanship were produced by the weavers of Scotland and Wales even after the Industrial Revolution had destroyed almost all village crafts in Britain. The initiators of the modern movement in the English textile industry . . . consciously transferred this unconscious tradition of exquisite weaving to the factory and carefully developed it there.[9]

The rediscovery of weaving in textile design during this period is well represented in the Industrial Art Collection. Many of the companies represented, including the Old Bleach Linen Company, Scottish Textile Weavers and Morton Sundour's experimental unit, Edinburgh Weavers, were Irish and Scottish based, where a sense of unbroken tradition was felt to have survived more or less intact. Old Bleach Linen drew upon the Irish linen tradition in their advertising material. While basically a traditional industry, weaving was peculiarly suited to Modernist theory, exploring texture through the use of different yarns and weaving processes, with pattern and surface decoration formed as a natural result of the weaving process. This idea of material and making dictating form and decoration was equally applicable to glass manufacture, in particular the firm of James Powell and Sons, with their simple rounded forms and use of colour conceived as a natural result of the glass-blowing process.

The exploration of formal values, particularly those illustrated by the relationship between old and new decorative arts, was another way into Pevsner's 'unconscious tradition'. This relationship was unexplored by Haward in spite of the good historic collections at Manchester City Art Gallery and the model of the Victoria and Albert Museum which collaborated with the Council for Art and Industry to mount a metalwork exhibition in 1934, and in 1935 'English Pottery Old and New'. This exhibition sought to 'illustrate the living tradition maintained in the art from medieval times to the present day', and had a broad remit, displaying industrially-produced domestic pottery, ceramics for factory use, and studio pottery alongside medieval earthenwares, eighteenth-century

Picotee teawares designed by John Adams and Harold Stabler for Carter, Stabler and Adams, acquired from the British Industrial Art Exhibition of 1933.

8   Harold Curwen, 'Perfection in Print' in John de Valette, *The Conquest of Ugliness*, London, 1934, pp.177–86.

9   Nikolaus Pevsner, ibid, p.55.

Lustre teawares by Gray's Pottery. This image was used extensively in the design press during the 1930s, and appeared in the *Pottery Gazette & Glass Trade Review* as late as 1944.

delftware, and even oriental ceramics as the inspiration for modern studio potters. In its juxtaposition of old and new, the exhibition display broke away from the evolutionary model of industrial art (with its disturbing legacy of Victorian chaos) and illustrated formal values, as W B Honey, the principal author of the exhibition leaflet, explained:

English pottery has always been distinguished by the devotion of its makers to utility as the prime reason for the existence of their ware: the virtues of these wares are generally the outcome of an intelligent use of their materials with this end in view, rather than any aim at deliberate effect.[10]

Thus tradition released from a time scale could be equated with Herbert Read's analogous examples of historical types. Read, reviewing the exhibition in *Architectural Review*, wrote approvingly of ' . . . *the return to tradition* . . . Now it may seem at first sight odd that we who are modernist without compromise should give voice to such an apparently reactionary cry. But we do so because we realize that the return to tradition is always the return to functional values.'[11]

Geoffrey Grigson, writing in *The Studio*, looked beyond this, adding the nationalist interpretation implicit in the exhibition's title. 'If there is (as I believe there is) an "Englishness" in our pottery, it would be a bad thing unless it were fairly elusive. If it were too obvious, down would smash the balance between the universal and the particular that every culture depends on . . .' Grigson's 'Englishness' was expressed in the aesthetic vocabulary of English pottery and led him to challenge Honey's statement of utility: 'The potter's motives cannot be so simply categorised; and I think it has pleased the English potter to build up on his wheel shapes which are graceful and robust in a naturalistic manner . . . Far the finest modern jug in the exhibition for form and quality of surface was a stoneware acid jug made by Messrs. Doulton . . . The tradition is still there in the factory, alive enough to be strengthened and extended . . .'[12]

Grigson found tradition in the maligned factory, a tradition that also expressed itself in laboratory glass, ginger-beer bottles, and Worcester laboratory dishes. In their anonymity of design, evolved to meet a functional need by nameless workers, wares such as these epitomised unconscious tradition. Doulton of Lambeth had developed acid-resistant stoneware in the 1830s, and a recognisable version of the 1930s jug appeared in the company's 1882 catalogue.[13] But by 1935 the jug had been 'discovered' by design reformers. Haward purchased a Doulton acid jug for the Manchester collection, and Doulton acid jugs – standing alone or ranked in order of size – featured prominently in Gordon Russell's new London showroom.

The jug's fashion status was based on contradictions and associations. In its subtle variations in form, the irregular surface

Typeface sheet donated by the Monotype Corporation in 1935.

Doulton & Co Ltd, Acid Jug, c.1935. Stoneware.
Industrial Art Collection,
Manchester City Art Gallery.

texture and the crudely finished and primitively styled strap handle, it combined the virtues of mass production with the cachet of the handmade and brought the aura of the factory to the living room but not the sterility. And although the jug was evolved for an impeccably utilitarian purpose, in the home it was almost functionless – a flower vase or umbrella stand. It was cheap, and theoretically available to all, although in reality it had limited appeal and, according to Pevsner, was stocked only by 'shops dealing in well-designed modern goods'.[14] Even at a superficial level its flaws were decorative, and the off-white body-colour harmonised with cream and beige interiors. A smaller version of the Doulton jug was produced by Gray's Pottery, a Staffordshire decorating firm consistently responsive to new trends. These were produced for industrial use by James Pearson of Chesterfield, and decorated by

[10] W B Honey, 'Introduction', *English Pottery Old and New*, London, 1935, p.5. (Honey is credited with authorship in the Victoria and Albert Museum archives. The exhibition dates were 15 April – 31 August 1935.)

[11] Herbert Read, 'Museum to the Rescue', *Architectural Review*, July 1935, pp.37–8.

[12] Geoffrey Grigson, 'In Search of English Pottery', *The Studio*, Vol 110, July–December 1935, pp.256–263, pp.256 and 258.

[13] September 1882. We are grateful to Alexander Clement for this reference.

[14] Nikolaus Pevsner, ibid, p.83.

Bernard Leach, Bowl, c 1936.
Stoneware with dark-green glaze.
York City Art Gallery (presented by the
Very Reverend Eric Milner-White,
Dean of York, 1959).

Gray's with brightly-coloured enamelled banding or abstract motifs. Haward acquired both Doulton and Gray's acid jugs for the Industrial Art Collection.

But for Bernard Leach, even Grigson's article, which looked beyond a tradition of continuity and utility and tried to get at a sense of an underlying collective expression of the national character, lacked a truly humanist dimension.

The artist's problem has now become the potter's problem – only genius solves it, whereas in old days simple innate race-genius did the work unknowingly. . . We can slip into an easy way of thinking the downright sensible qualities of Doulton's & Bourne's technical wares as aesthetic as those of old English or Chinese pots from a natural desire to take pride in any art born unostentatiously of our age. The fact is, one cannot say more of these pots than that they are honest and sensible. They have not much sensitiveness, or quality, and cannot possibly be expected to have such . . .[15]

The Doulton acid jug and other stoneware by Fulham Pottery and Joseph Bourne (Denby), terracotta jugs and natural weaves survived in spartan modern interiors because they were sanctioned by continuity and functionalism. But they also provided textural contrast, and more abstractly, in the counterpoint of old and new. Antiques, although widely collected and often visible in interiors published in the *Studio Yearbook*, during the mid-1930s at least were rarely admitted to be desirable. Gordon Russell, writing in 1934, sounded tentative:

. . . it may prove useful to have one or two beautifully designed and handmade pieces of furniture – antiques if you like – in a room which is

[15] Bernard Leach, letter, *The Studio*, Vol. 111, January–June 1936, p.119.

[16] Gordon Russell, 'The Living Room and Furniture Design' in John Gloag (ed.), *Design in Modern Life*, London, 1934, pp.39–46, p.46.

[17] Herbert Read, *Staffordshire Pottery Figures*, London, 1929, p.22.

otherwise furnished by the machine. The two techniques of making are quite different and both in a properly-balanced world should be good.[16]

Equally undiscussed, at least by design reformers, was the collecting of popular historic decorative art, as an expression of 'unconscious tradition'. Read wrote of Staffordshire flat-back figures in 1929: 'The potter who made the figure was himself a peasant with a simple mind and a simple sense of humour. But because of this simple sense he often strays unconsciously into a realm of purer forms. He blunders into beauty . . .'[17]

This abstraction made such art acceptable and led to some oddly-assorted room interiors. A sparsely-furnished bedroom in Lubetkin's and Tecton's Modernist block of flats, Highpoint, illustrated by

Vase designed by Keith Murray for Stevens & Williams, acquired from the British Industries Fair in 1939.

'Chale', linen crash, designed by Eva Crofts for Donald Brothers, acquired from the British Industries Fair in 1937.

Yorke and Gibberd, included a pair of Staffordshire flat-back dogs either side of a divan bed.[18]

By 1937, Pevsner was regretting a resurgence of period reproductions, but Haward preferred modernity and did not collect reproductions or even revivalist pieces. However, the Industrial Art Collection does include a number of pieces with peasant motifs of the type associated with the art pottery movement of the early twentieth century, but current well into the 1930s. A superficially-naive and cheerful approach to colour and a bold sense of pattern characterised the freely-painted motifs of Gray's and Poole Pottery, and even Susie Cooper's banded tableware shared this bold sense of colour, combining it with an overtly 'functional' style of decoration. Textile manufacturers Donald Brothers produced a number of textiles designed by Eva Crofts, sister of Dame Laura Knight, decorated

Pillar. Barbara Hepworth for Edinburgh Weavers. The Whitworth Art Gallery, University of Manchester.

Aircraft. Marion Dorn for Old Bleach Linen Co.
The Whitworth Art Gallery,
University of Manchester.

with large-scale floral prints in one or two bright colours on a textured buff ground. Although a superficial expression of 'unconscious tradition', cheerful, free designs such as these were broadly acceptable to the design reformers, as a way of gradually educating the public to appreciate simplicity of form and design.

Of course tradition was not always good. Pevsner wrote gloomily of the survival of the bad tradition of glass cutting in the glass trade. There was also the relative stagnation of design in silver and porcelain, buyers preferring to offset the expense of purchase against the expectation of infrequent replacement. Design reformers frequently lamented the conservatism of the British public, with its phlegmatic reliance on an image of 'Olde Englande' to sell its goods abroad, and its cautious buying habits at home. Pevsner, the foreigner, wrote: 'Britain's greatness appears inseparable from Britain's conservatism . . . However while this basic English quality accounts for a certain hesitation in the adoption of the Modern Movement,

[18] F R S Yorke and Frederick Gibberd, *The Modern Flat*, London, originally published 1937, 1948 edition, p.87. This was Lubetkin's own flat.

Keith Murray, Cactus Vase for Stevens &
Williams, c.1935. Lead crystal, engraved.
Broadfield House Glass Museum.

Keith Murray, Fish Vase for Stevens & Williams,
c.1935. Lead crystal, engraved.
Broadfield House Glass Museum.

the modern style in its entirety cannot be one of those which
England will in the long run refuse. For it is a simple and rational
style, and moreover a style in the creation of which England has had
a considerable share . . . In finally adopting the modern style as it
was developed abroad, England is only recovering what she once
gave the world.'[19]

But Morris was a difficult figure, for although appreciated as a
visionary thinker, his ideals of a pre-machine society had engen-
dered a precious arty-craftiness that Britain was still trying to shake
off, and the realisation of his ideals entailed an apocalyptic reorder-
ing of society. Craftsmen who stood outside the major producers
had little future as significant economic contributors, and Gropius's
concept of craft as a laboratory for mass-production was frequently
cited as a way forward. Pevsner gave the example of Morton Sundour and the Edinburgh Weavers – well represented in the Manchester Industrial Art Collection. If the basic model was good, there
was no reason why it should be affected by mass-production. Certainly Haward was not fully committed to modern craft; the
Manchester craft collection, intended to parallel the Industrial Art

Collection, was smaller, of lower quality – accessions money was scarce – and collected locally unlike his industrial art.

But a positive legacy of the Arts and Crafts Movement was still strong in many British decorative arts. James Powell and Sons (Whitefriars) continued to make glass in the arts and crafts shapes that had established its reputation for high-quality design during the nine-teenth century. In the 1930s, this reputation was maintained by a range of glass that relied upon simplicity and grace of form. The self-confidence of an intimate understanding of British tradition enabled Powell to produce a stylistically-broad range of glass – a refined arts and crafts style alongside neo-Georgian designs, and cut glass patterns in both historical and 'jazz modern' styles.

Haward began his collection at a time when Britain appeared to be on the threshold of making a significant contribution to Modernism. He stopped collecting in 1939, after nearly ten years of ultimately disappointing endeavour that paralleled the experience of design reformers more widely, and the collection was not revived after the war. Many of the plainer pre-war designs, such as Keith Murray's ceramics and the Edinburgh Weavers' textiles, continued to

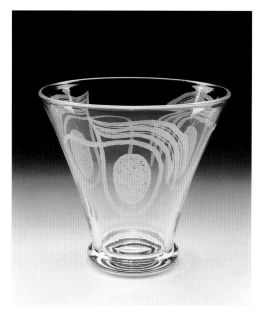

Graham Sutherland, Vase for Stuart & Sons, 1934. Lead crystal, blown and engraved. Broadfield House Glass Museum (Hulbert of Dudley Collection).

Graham Sutherland, Vase for Stuart & Sons, 1934. Lead crystal, blown and cut. Broadfield House Glass Museum (Hulbert of Dudley Collection).

[19] Nikolaus Pevsner, *ibid.*, pp.204–5.

be made and admired well into the 1950s. Other more populist designs, such as Susie Cooper's Kestrel shaped wares, were criticised by writers such as Bernard Hollowood after the war for mannerisms of style, but were equally enduring.[20] They were legacies of the more practical awareness of Modernism that had emerged during the 1930s. As early-1930s Modernism was recognised to be merely a

William Staite Murray, Jar: 'Motet for Strings', 1937–9. Stoneware with iron glaze and incised and brushed decoration. York City Gallery (presented by the Very Reverend Eric Milner-White, Dean of York, 1963).

stylist's Modernism of clinical interiors, minimal decoration and obsessive streamlining, so tradition had offered an acceptable way forward and fuelled the Georgian revival of the late 1930s. It was more than dressing up Modernism and selling it to the conservative British public. Tradition provided the human face of Modernism, civilising but also sentimental and, in its refinement of activities, instinctive to all men, universal rather than particular.[21] It transcended nationalism, drawing upon the commonality of nationalist preoccupations – whether they were Swedish, German, or even an American consciousness defined by its 'newness'. Haward's Industrial Art Collection was in many ways a personal collection, but in its

Opposite page:
William Staite Murray, Tall Jar: 'The Bather', 1930. Stoneware with cream glaze, decorated with bands in ironrust red and cobalt. York City Art Gallery (presented by the Very Reverend Eric Milner-White, Dean of York, 1959).

[20] Bernard Hollowood, *Pottery and Glass*, London, 1947.
[21] See especially Herbert Read, 'Towards a Duplex Civilisation' in *The Grass Roots of Art*, London, 1955 pp.130–57.

Gray's Pottery, Banded Jar, 1935.
Industrial Art Collection,
Manchester City Art Gallery.

broadness of scope it illustrates the many different strands of British Modernism in the decorative arts.

It is a mistake, I repeat, to assume that art must all be of one pattern, even within one period or one civilisation. The sacred and the profane have always existed side by side in human destiny, and on that analogy we might suppose a machine art and a human art could exist side by side. It is even possible that a reciprocity would then be established between man's intellectual and sensuous faculties which would lead to a culture of an order altogether higher than any hitherto attained in the world's history.

Herbert Read [22]

Covered goblet, designed by Barnaby Powell for James Powell & Sons (Whitefriars Ltd), acquired from the British Industries Fair in 1935.

[22] Herbert Read, introduction to *The Practice of Design*, London, 1946, pp.9–21, p.21.

The Englishness of English Art

JUDITH COLLINS

This essay examines some aspects of the Modern Movement in England that were particular to this country and different from contemporary concerns in mainland Europe during the 1930s. In this decade there was a growing tendency among English artists and critics to examine the nature of their art and to identify its strengths. The previous decade of the 1920s had been one of retrenchment and insularity, with young artists concentrating on the genres of still life and landscape in a loose, painterly fashion. The formalist aesthetics of Roger Fry and Clive Bell were still prominent. No new styles or manifestos burst forth and there was not much evidence of keeping abreast with European developments. At the beginning of the 1930s this sense of insularity became a motivating power. National culture had to be identified so that it could be nurtured, cherished and protected against invasion. But it was not there to stifle or limit creativity; it was there to encourage and inspire. There was a strong interest in early English art, particularly Celtic artefacts and Anglo-Saxon and Romanesque paintings and sculpture. Two critics, Herbert Read and Stanley Casson, made interesting comparisons between the art of their own day and that of earlier centuries, and at least three artists did the same: Paul Nash, John Piper and William Johnstone.

Paul Nash started to write art criticism for the *Weekend Review* and *The Listener* in 1930, and as a painter and critic he was well placed to reflect on the characteristics and merits of English art in the context of the European avant-garde. He wrote an article for the *Weekend Review*, published on 12 March 1932, with the title 'Going Modern and being British', and in this Nash enquired whether it was possible to do both. Going modern meant taking on board and incorporating into one's own work European developments of the later 1920s, such as the paintings of Picasso, Braque, Miró and Arp, while being British meant being true to one's roots. Nash concluded that it was possible to combine both approaches. He was the driving force behind the

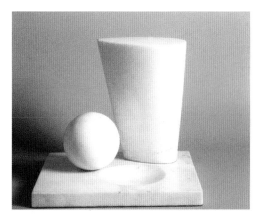

Barbara Hepworth, *Conoid, Sphere and Hollow II*, 1937. Marble. Government Art Collection.

formation in June 1933 of Unit One, a group of eleven contemporary English painters, sculptors and architects: Moore, Hepworth, Armstrong, Bigge, Burra, Hillier, Nash himself, Nicholson, Wadsworth, Wells Coates and Colin Lucas. The formation of this loose group was strategic; it was to announce both in a national and an international arena that something new was happening in English art. A book of statements by Unit One members was published in April 1934, and Nash's text posed the question: 'To what extent has contemporary art in England a national character ? . . . Can we find in our short history of painting and of sculpture, qualities so peculiar as to identify their subjects beyond doubt, and, if so, do these qualities persist today?' He answered by distinguishing the dominant tendency which has recurred throughout the history of English art as 'a pronounced linear method in design, no doubt traceable to sources in Celtic ornament'.

Three years later Nash returned to his examination of the Englishness of English art and extended it beyond Celtic linearity. In an article called 'A Characteristic', published in the *Architectural Record* in March 1937, he was still concerned with what it was that defined a:

natural inspiration, something whose lineaments seemed almost redolent of place and time within the limits of these shores. A thing one might describe, in no parochial sense, as English . . . We have been accustomed too long and slavishly to accept the prejudice of our connoisseurs and pedagogues whose

Edward McKnight Kauffer, *Actors Prefer Shell*, 1935. Poster: The Shell Art Collection.

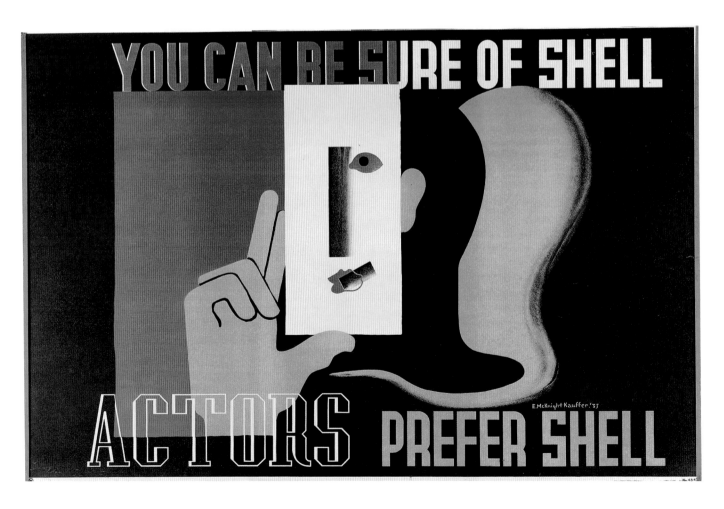

TO VISIT BRITAIN'S LANDMARKS

BRIMHAM ROCK, YORKSHIRE   GRAHAM SUTHERLAND

YOU CAN BE SURE OF SHELL

Graham Sutherland, *Brimham Rock, Yorkshire,*
1937. Poster: The Shell Art Collection.

understanding, for the most part, is at fault. Either they would have us
believe that English art is essentially artless or that its formal expression is
almost entirely derivative. Neither suggestion is true . . . I have found abun-
dant evidence that throughout the short history of English art not only does
inspiration glow as though renewed by some constant spring, but in every age
and in every field of invention the same lively qualities of interpretation are
present . . . it is time that the cloud of false witness was rolled away to make
space for an intelligent illumination of the very distinct features of our true
countenance.

Nash then chose illustrations of a range of paintings, architecture
and ancient sites which all displayed an 'architectonic quality' found
in the best English art, prominent among which were the great
stone circle at Stonehenge and Silbury Hill in Wiltshire, and the
ramparts of a stone age fort called Maiden Castle in Dorset. Stonehenge was 'a religious monument without parallel'; Maiden Castle
showed a 'most formidable and perfect example of hill architecture'
while the landscape around Silbury Hill was 'almost *Surreal* with its
unprepared approach to the abrupt intrusion of a hill of such vast
proportions'. All these he remarked, 'seem to me the symbols of our
formal heritage. From their influence flowed out the inspiration of
the early sculptors, the makers of the Saxon fonts and crosses.' Nash
ended his article with stirring words: 'it is obvious that with the
complete decline of Impressionism and the exposure of the Pre-
Raphaelite myth, English art has begun to grow into a healthy shape
again'. He appeared here to be reclaiming his heritage, a mix of
formal abstraction and Surrealism, from Neolithic and Saxon times
and using it to forge new work. He first discovered the 'wonderful
and disquieting' triple stone circles at Avebury in July 1933 and was
overwhelmed by their formal drama and their setting. In his Unit
One statement he made an enigmatic confession: 'Last summer I
walked in a field near Avebury where two rough stone monoliths

stand up, sixteen feet high, miraculously patterned with black and orange lichen . . . A mile away, a green pyramid casts a gigantic shadow. In the hedge at hand, the white trumpet of a convolvulus turns from its spiral stem, following the sun. In my art I would solve such an equation.' Between 1934 and 1938 Nash painted several oils and watercolours on the subject of Avebury and its stone megaliths,

Eric Gill, *Ariel hearing Celestial Music*, 1931. Bath stone relief. The Chairman and Board of Governors of the BBC.

Eric Gill, *Ariel between Wisdom and Gaiety*, 1931. Bath stone relief. The Chairman and Board of Governors of the BBC.

and the nearby mound of Silbury Hill. Each was a synthesis of naturalistic observation and expressive abstraction.

The young German art historian, Nikolaus Pevsner, whose specialisations included Italian Baroque painting and German Baroque architecture, came to England at the beginning of the 1930s and began to accumulate material for a book on the national characteristics of English art, stimulated by the constrast in depth of his professional knowledge of European art and that of the unknown country which welcomed him. This research was eventually published in 1955 with the title *The Englishness of English Art*, although Pevsner gave a lecture series on the subject at Birkbeck College, London, during 1941–2. One of Pevsner's lectures was called 'Blake and the Flaming Line'. Pevsner found that Blake used line in a tender, tense, flowing and flaming manner and 'where energy rather than abandon is intended, he forces figures into an imposed abstract geometry'. Blake's interest in line was traced back to the 'illuminated manuscripts of the seventh and eighth centuries in Northumberland as well as Ireland, and perhaps, though more hesitatingly, to the style of the Celtic Britons in England in the Iron Age, the spiral scrolls decorating the Desborough Mirror at the British Museum and the [Battersea] shield from the Thames in the same collection'. Pevsner's conclusions about the Englishness of English art were similar to those of Nash, but he stopped short of comparing earlier art with that of his own time.

Nash was not the only artist to compare modern art with Anglo-Saxon and Celtic work. John Piper also used this device to justify the avant-garde developments of his own era. He wrote an article entitled 'England's Early Sculptors' which was published in *Architectural Review* in October 1936, and was richly illustrated with his own and Myfanwy Evans's photographs of English Romanesque carved stone capitals and fonts. Piper's text drew comparisons with avant-garde artists of his own day and those of Anglo-Saxon and Romanesque times: 'From the eighth century onwards for about five hundred years sculptors were dealing with forms very like those used by artists in our time working in the light of (or reacting from) the achievement of Cézanne, Seurat and the Cubists. The purely non-figurative artists of some early Northumbrian and Cornish crosses were the forbears of the pure abstractionists of today. There were also early reactions against recognised forms, and obvious expressions of the subconscious, that find a contemporary parallel in Surrealism. The Picasso-like profile on the font at Morville [Shropshire] could have had a comfortable place in the International Surrealist Exhibition. Up to the end of the twelfth century there was a strong bias towards geometric forms, and purely abstract pattern had an important function in any decorative scheme. Figure sculpture grew out of abstract pattern, and retired back into it at intervals – single early examples with animals and figures embroiled in the surrounding patterns often resemble the rare birds hatching with many forebodings from a Max Ernst egg . . . It is certain that side by side with the work of sculptors like Brancusi, Arp and Moore, and painters like Picasso, Kandinsky, Klee and Miró, these works are full of meaning for the present day. The local type of carving to be seen on the font at Toller Fratrum, Dorset . . . has the bigness and strangeness that has been accessory to so much of the achievement of Picasso, and through him and others to the aesthetic revelations of the twentieth century.'

Piper then wrote a second article which dealt with the rediscovery of English culture of previous centuries and compared it with the

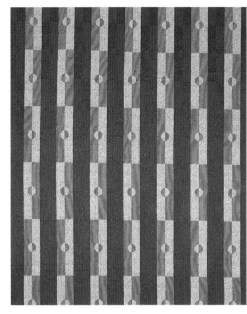

Attributed to Ben Nicholson, Fabric Length for Edinburgh Weavers. Target Gallery, London.

Edward McKnight Kauffer, *Stonehenge*, 1931.
Poster: The Shell Art Collection.

present; this was 'Prehistory from the Air' which was published in his wife's avant-garde magazine *Axis* in 1937. Aerial photographs for use in archaeological investigations had been instituted at the end of the First World War. Two men, O G S Crawford and Alexander Keiller, spent time and money in the 1920s and 1930s and produced a series of splendid, sharp and detailed aerial photographs of ancient sites in Wessex which had a huge influence on archaeological theory and practice. Piper was enchanted by their photographs and moved enough to write this article, which explained that current aesthetic perception had changed as a result. 'Flying (whether we do it ourselves or not) has changed our sense of spaces and forms and vistas enormously . . . The significant thing being that from the air *horizons vanish* . . . It has also vanished (nearly) from painting. Instead of being the end-all of landscape, it is now there on sufferance . . . At its simplest, the change is one from elevation to plan. The picture has tipped over backwards on to the floor, and in being raised again it has brought part of the floor with it. Picasso, Braque, Klee, Matisse have painted elevations of wineglasses, gardens and windows at Nice which have the added richness and meaning of plan-patterns.' The illustrations which accompanied the article were line drawings from William Stukeley's *Stonehenge* and *Avebury* of 1724, Colt Hoare's *Ancient Wiltshire* of 1812, juxtaposed with aerial photographs of Wiltshire and a recent painting by Miró. Piper's own paintings in the mid-1930s narrowed down from an interest in recording topography to one charged with an ordering of coloured patterns and shapes, and for a short while his work was exclusively abstract. The Neolithic, Anglo-Saxon and Romanesque work that Piper admired and wrote about was concerned with primary forms such as circles and lozenges and his own art for a short while mirrored that.

Neolithic, Iron Age and Bronze Age burial mounds, stone circles and other sites in southern England, particularly those in Wiltshire and Dorset, were at the forefront of interest in the national heritage in the 1930s. In August 1927, an appeal was launched to restore and preserve the open surroundings of Stonehenge for the nation, headed by Stanley Baldwin, the Prime Minister. The purchase was completed by 1929 and the land was vested in the National Trust. By the early 1930s more than 15,000 visitors arrived by charabanc each summer month. Jack Beddington, promotions manager for Shell petrol in the 1930s, commissioned a poster of Stonehenge from Edward McKnight Kauffer. At the same time Alexander Keiller, who lived in the village of Avebury, was excavating, restoring and preserving Avebury at his own expense, as well as involving himself in the world of aerial photography. Mortimer Wheeler carried out excavations at Maiden Castle near Dorchester in the summers of 1934 and 1935, and Nash took photographs of the excavated skeletons of the Ancient Britons who fell in battle against the Roman invaders. The Ordnance Survey produced its first map of Britain in the Dark Ages in 1935. Three Bronze Age barrows outside Woodbridge in Suffolk were excavated in the summers of 1938 and 1939 and the Sutton Hoo treasure of gold and garnets, the richest hoard ever dug from English soil, was brought to light and given to the nation on 23 August 1939, two weeks before the British Declaration of War against Nazi Germany.

Edward Wadsworth, *Pen Pits*, 1936.
Oil on canvas. Private collection.

The painter William Johnstone was not one of the members of Unit One, nor one of the leading figures in avant-garde London circles. However, he studied under Andre L'Hote in Paris in the 1920s and was therefore very well informed about the newest developments in European art. He returned to London in 1929 and took up a teaching post in Hackney. He was commissioned to write a book called *Creative Art in England From the Earliest Times to the Present* which was published by the Art Book Club in 1936. Johnstone presented 'the character of the most intense and creative English work, using the method of comparison', and, like Piper, set two comparative illustrations side by side: a contemporary painting by Picasso and an embossed silver plate made in Hexham, Northumbria, in the midninth century. Johnstone's book began with English art of the fifth century and the Anglo-Saxon invasions. England then became ' a vortex of ideas' and this 'provided an atmosphere in which vital work could grow . . . The outstanding feature of this early Anglo-

Henry Moore, *Reclining Figure*, 1931. Bronze.
The Henry Moore Foundation: gift of the artist,
1977. Photograph: Michael Muller.

Saxon work is its abstract quality. It does not attempt to represent in a naturalistic visual manner but rather formalises significant features selected through emotional experiences and re-created in expressive design and shape.' Although this sentence described art of a much earlier century, it is remarkably similar to the way Herbert Read wrote about the avant-garde art of his own time. Johnstone was born on the Scottish-English border and his perspective on English art has a Scottish flavour to it. While he was a student in Paris and looking for his own individual style, he reflected on his northern heritage: 'I remembered the great Celtic and Saxon carvings; I remembered the Book of Kells and the Lindisfarne Gospels; I remembered the Bewcastle and Ruthwell crosses, the Burghhead Bull, St Cuthbert's coffin in Durham. I realized that, in the early Northern art, there was something for me.' This 'something' was an appreciation of the expressive abstract geometry of Celtic and Saxon art. In his autobiography *Points in Time*, written in 1980, Johnstone remembered how much pleasure he gained from his visits to the Anglo-Saxon section of the British Museum in the 1930s: 'At the back of a case containing a jumbled collection of Anglo-Saxon tools I saw a marvellous ornamental mace-head of white chalcedony, carved with the greatest sensitivity as well as mathematical precision, a carving which would have inspired the envy of Brancusi.'

Herbert Read wrote an article titled 'English Art' for the December 1933 issue of the *Burlington Magazine*, and in this he attempted, like Nash and Pevsner, 'to define the essential characteristics of English art'. Read argued that the first distinct style 'to be distinctly English was formed during the so-called Anglo-Saxon period' and that 'this style has for its main characteristic a certain calligraphic or linear freedom'. But he also found that 'the absolute qualities of grace and rhythm conveyed by the linear conventions' were combined with

Opposite page:
Henry Moore, *Stringed Figure*. Bowl, 1938.
Bronze and string.
The Henry Moore Foundation:
gift of the artist, 1979.

John Skeaping, *Akua-Ba*, 1931. Acacia wood.
Private collection.

'what Ruskin, in rather shocked tones, called "our earthly instinct"'.
Both qualities, Read noted, could be found side by side in a sym-
biotic relationship on the pages of English illuminated manuscripts
from the eighth to the thirteenth centuries, but after that they
seemed to go their separate ways. The major aesthetic discussion
among English artists at the end of the 1920s and into the 1930s was
the choice between practising art of an illustrative, anecdotal or
psychological nature or that of an austere, abstract formal kind – the
two strands of English art identified by Read. Both kinds could be
found among the artists of Unit One.

By 1939 the excitement in English cultural circles over the rediscovery
and promotion of Celtic, Anglo-Saxon and Romanesque art evaporated.
Comparisons between Picasso and seventh century Northumbrian engraved plaques, or between Brancusi and a marble Anglo-Saxon mace
head, seemed no longer valid as the world turned its attention to more
sombre issues. The Englishness of English Art was a topic that went
underground and remained buried for several decades.

Isokon

ALASTAIR GRIEVE

Isokon[1] is the name of a firm which was set up in December 1931. The directors were Molly Pritchard, a bacteriologist, Graham Maw, a solicitor, and Robert S Spicer, an economist. But the two most important people, who for professional reasons did not become directors, were Molly Pritchard's husband, Jack, and the architect Wells Coates. The name was a composite one derived by Jack Pritchard from the term 'Isometric Unit Construction'. It was intended that the firm should make houses, flats, furniture and fittings in units and these were to be designed by Wells Coates who was fond of using Isometric drawings. Pritchard was to act as consultant.

Wells Coates and the Pritchards had met in 1929. They found they shared ideas about solutions to the problems of modern city living for busy professional people. In August of the following year they set up the firm of Wells Coates and Partners to build and equip two model unit houses on a plot of land in Lawn Road, Belsize Park, bought by the Pritchards in 1929. These houses were to be occupied by themselves but they were envisaged as prototypes which would embody their ideas of unit construction, built-in furniture and the latest equipment designed to make life simpler. This firm's name was changed to Isokon at Pritchard's suggestion because it was felt to be professionally improper for Wells Coates to be employed by a firm with his own name.

Wells made some designs for these *Isotype dwellings* in Lawn Road, but he and the Pritchards soon felt that the houses would not provide a real solution to the problems they wanted to solve. So in the spring of 1932 the Pritchards gave Wells Coates a brief for a block of service flats instead of houses on the land. By June of the following year, the project was far enough advanced for a full-size model of a complete flat to be shown at an exhibition, *British Industrial Art in Relation to the Home,* at Dorland Hall in Lower Regent Street. It was favourably received and the long list of prospective tenants gained then enabled Jack Pritchard, who was not a wealthy

Wells Coates, Lawn Road Flats.
Photograph: British Architectural Library, RIBA, London.

Notes

[1] Many of the facts used are taken from a paper on Isokon read by Jack Pritchard to the School of Fine Arts, University of East Anglia, Norwich, on 30 May 1973. Otherwise the material is largely drawn from the Pritchard Archive at the University of East Anglia.

Lawn Road Flats: standard dressing room.
Photogaph: Jack Pritchard Archive,
University of East Anglia.

man, to raise the money to build. A memorandum by him, dated 3 July 1933 and written in connection with this, deserves to be quoted at length as it explains the *Isokon Idea*:

1.Isokon is a proprietary word that I have coined to denote the application of modern functional design to houses, flats, furniture and fittings. It implies also the idea of building in variety from standard units.

2.What I have in mind is, first of all, to build and manage a number of Isokon service flats and set up each flat with Isokon furniture and fittings. Later on, I would apply the same Isokon idea to the building of private houses to householders' specifications. Such houses would be built from Isokon units in accordance with Isokon principles. Each householder would be a potential customer for Isokon furniture and fittings. It is believed that there is a growing interest in modern design and appreciation of its common-sense economy. I don't think it would be difficult to make the word synonymous with modern design in relation to homes.[2]

Permission to erect the flats was given by London County Council, after some delay, on 16 September 1933, and they were opened on 9 July 1934. The Pritchards themselves moved into a small flat on the roof of the building completed some months later. They lined the walls of their flat with plywood panelling designed by Wells Coates and furnished it with the latest metal-tube furniture designed by Aalto, Breuer and others, which they bought from a Zurich firm early in October 1934.

Agatha Christie, who lived for a time during the war in the Lawn Road Flats, likened them to a giant liner moored against a bank of trees. Today they still demand attention. They are so boldly sculptural and at the same time they seem so logically conceived. In a short speech given on the opening day, Molly Pritchard said that the first question they asked themselves was: 'How do we want to live, what sort of framework must we build round ourselves to make that living as pleasant as possible?'[3] The flats provided an answer for young professional people with incomes of between £250 and £500 per annum who would otherwise be condemned to the misery of living in digs. The basic functions of living – cooking, washing, dressing, sleeping – were thoughtfully provided for in the planning of each flat, and tenants could make use of services such as meals and laundry if they wished. As the flats were fully equipped with storage space and necessary items of furniture, all the tenants needed to bring with them were their light personal belongings. In an interview published in *The Listener* on 24 May 1933, Wells Coates described the approach to life which lay behind his planning:

We cannot burden ourselves with permanent tangible possessions, as well as with our real new possessions of freedom, travel, new experience – in short, what we call 'life'.[4]

What had led the Pritchards and Wells Coates to these ideas? Jack Pritchard was born into an old Hampstead family in 1899. He had served

² Pritchard archive.

³ Pritchard archive.

⁴ 'Modern Dwellings for Modern Needs': a discussion between Geoffrey Boumphrey and Wells Coates, *The Listener*, 24 May 1933, p.819.

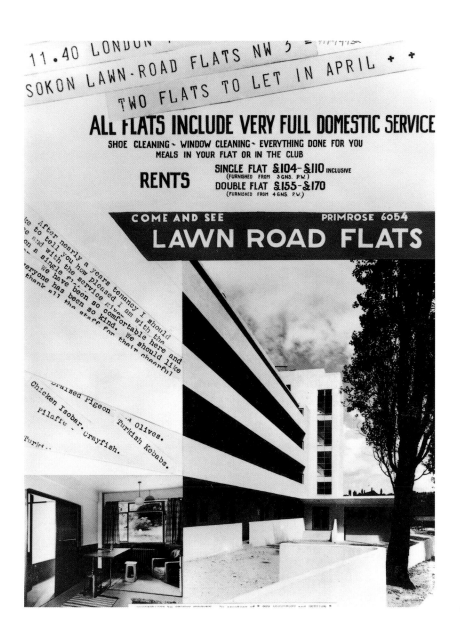

Early advertisement for Lawn Road Flats.
Jack Pritchard Archive, University of East Anglia.

in the Royal Navy in the First World War before taking a degree in Engineering and Economics at Cambridge. There he had been impressed by Keynes' condemnation of the way the peace terms with Germany were being whittled away and also, and in the long term to a greater extent, by the ideas of Henry Morris who in 1922 became County Education Secretary for Cambridgeshire. Morris wanted Pritchard to take a job with social relevance but, when Pritchard left Cambridge in the summer of that year, he went to learn scientific management with the Michelin Tyre Company in Clermont-Ferrand. In 1924 he married Molly who had taken a science degree at Cambridge and then a medical qualification in London, and in September 1925 he took up another job, with his duties deliberately left undefined, with the Venesta Plywood Company. In that year he visited the International Decorative Arts Exhibition in Paris, but he does not seem to have become aware, fully, of the Modern Movement on the Continent until some years later.

Pritchard became very much involved with Venesta. The firm's factories, run by the Luther family at Tallin in Estonia, had pio-

neered the development of plywood and adhesives, but Pritchard found that Venesta was using plywood more as a substitute for solid wood than for its intrinsic qualities, which were its lightness, strength and its capacity to be formed into curves. Towards the late 1920s he saw that the solution lay in the functional and aesthetic ideas evolved by Le Corbusier in Paris and by Gropius and his colleagues at the Bauhaus in Germany. While working for Venesta in Paris in 1929–30, Pritchard saw Le Corbusier's work at first hand, visiting houses such as Les Terraces at Garches and, with the encouragement of John Gloag who worked in an advertising agency employed by Venesta, he got Le Corbusier, together with Pierre Jeanneret and Charlotte Perriand, to design a stand for Venesta at the Building Trades Exhibition, held at Olympia in September 1930. In October, Charlotte Perriand sent him a collection of photographs of interiors by Le Corbusier, and sometime in this year the Pritchards and Wells Coates went to Stuttgart to look at the suburb of modern houses built by Mies van der Rohe, Gropius, Le Corbusier and others at the Weissenhof in 1927. While in Paris, Pritchard also met the Russian architect Lubetkin who was shortly to come to England and form the Tecton group. In March 1931, Pritchard went to Germany again with Serge Chermayeff and Wells Coates. They saw the Bauhaus at Dessau and met Eric Mendelsohn in Berlin, who showed them round his own house and his Metal Workers' Union Building.

By this date Jack Pritchard had started to play an active part in various groups interested in the reform of British design. He had been introduced to the Design and Industries Association (DIA) by John Gloag and in 1933 became chairman of its Council. The President of the DIA was Frank Pick, the enlightened General Manager of London Transport, and he gave Pritchard advice on the financing of Lawn Road Flats. With the encouragement of Maxwell Fry, the DIA also supported the idea of showing a Minimum Flat at the Dorland Hall Exhibition. In July 1930, Pritchard joined the Cambridge architectural theorist, Mansfield Forbes, together with Chermayeff, Howard Robertson and Wells Coates, in the Twentieth Century Group which was interested in forming a new attitude to furniture and equipment in the home. In 1931–2 he worked with Maxwell Fry, Wells Coates and others on a scheme for an exhibition of Planned Industrial Construction to be held at the Building Trades Exhibition in September 1932. Planning was thought to be the answer to the troubled economic situation after the 1929 slump, and EPIC set out 'to demonstrate to the business man, the architect and the builder, the waste of not planning ahead and, conversely, the economy and profit to be gained by Planned Industrial Construction.'[5]

It aimed to show the advantages of a well-planned factory and surroundings with transport, workers' housing and amenities integrated in the development. Other planning schemes in which

Isokon Stacking Stool, c.1933.
Birch plywood.
University of East Anglia Collection.
Photograph: Michael Brandon-Jones.

Opposite page:
Wells Coates, Isokon Electric Fire, 1934.
Plywood, copper faced.
University of East Anglia Collection.
Photograph: Michael Brandon-Jones.

[5] From a memorandum on EPIC dated 25 November 1931 in Jack Pritchard's possession.

Pritchard was concerned at this time were Political and Economic Planning (PEP) and Tecplan, which aimed to cut across political parties and produce a shared planning policy. Tecplan produced an impressive booklet called *A View on Planning* in December 1933 which 'intended to sketch within manageable compass and in plain terms, the problem of planning as a whole, in its political, social, economic and psychological bearings' (page 4).

Wells Coates was engaged with Pritchard on several of these projects.[6] When they met in 1929, Pritchard had been attracted by the way Coates used plywood in shops he was remodelling for the Cresta firm. The light screens, fitted cupboards and drawers with simple metal handles in these shops provided a model for the storage equipment in the Lawn Road Flats. A shared interest in the design of new storage space, which would make houses easier to keep clean, drew the Pritchards and Wells Coates together. By the time they met, the Pritchards had already had a large fitted wardrobe installed in a house at 79 Platts Lane, where they lived from 1927, and their move from this address in 1929 and a succession of further moves before they settled into their flat in Lawn Road, must have led them to agree wholeheartedly with Wells's expressed belief that 'Very soon it will be considered quite as fantastic to move accompanied by wardrobes, tables and beds, as it would seem today to remove the bath, or the heating-system including the pipes.'[7]

Wells Coates's enthusiasm for built-in storage space had its roots in the traditional architecture of Japan, where he was born in 1895 and where he spent his childhood. His parents were Canadians and shortly before the war he started a degree course in Structural and Mechanical Engineering at McGill University. He served as a pilot during the war and completed his studies at McGill in 1922. Following this he did research in England on 'The Gas Temperature of the Diesel Cycle' for which he received a PhD in 1924. In the next year he was working as a translator in Paris and it was then that he became aware of modern French painting and design. In 1927, while furnishing a flat for his family, he realised that he had a gift for the designing of uncluttered living areas and compact storage space. The firm of Cresta took him on in 1929 and he did several shops for them and a factory at Welwyn in 1931. Through the Twentieth Century Group and Mansfield Forbes, he was invited to design sound studios for the new BBC building in Portland Place in 1932. In these studios he used metal tube furniture and took care not to disguise the beauty of functional electrical equipment.

Following his meeting with Pritchard, Wells Coates designed three display stands for Venesta. For the first of these (in the winter of 1930–1) which won first prize in an open competition, Wells submitted an Isometric design under the pseudonym *Isoplan*. The stands were, of course, built of plywood and they had to draw

[6] The most informative study of Wells Coates is the PhD thesis by F H Elgohary, 'Wells Coates and his position in the beginning of the modern movement', University of London, 1966.

[7] Wells Coates, 'Materials for Architecture', *Architects' Journal*, 4 November 1931, p.588.

Wells Coates, PEL Typist's Desk.
Tubular steel and black-stained wood.
Target Gallery, London.

attention to themselves. In them, Wells Coates was able to experiment with the bold sculptural forms he was shortly to realise in concrete in the Lawn Road Flats. To some extent they enabled him to make up for his lack of real building experience, but it was nevertheless a very brave decision of the Pritchards to let him go ahead on the large and unconventional structure of the flats.

At the time of the design and erection of the flats, Wells Coates was also involved in the formation of two other important groups: Unit One and MARS. Unit One was an association of eleven painters, sculptors and architects including Nash, Nicholson, Wadsworth, Hepworth, Moore, Colin Lucas, and Coates himself, who possibly suggested the group's name. In a letter to *The Times* of 2 June 1933, announcing the group's formation, Nash remarked that 'Unit One may be said to stand for the expression of a truly contemporary spirit, for that thing which is recognised as peculiarly of today in painting, sculpture and architecture.' Their publication, *Unit One – the Modern Movement in English architecture, painting and sculpture,* edited by Herbert Read, appeared in 1934. It contained an 'axonometric' drawing of the Lawn Road Flats and a credo by Wells. Here he stressed that the economic and social problems of the day, and not the styles of the past, had to guide the architect in his attempts to produce 'a formal aspect of order and significance'.

Serge Chermayeff, Cabinet.
Target Gallery, London.

Opening day at Lawn Road Flats: 9 July 1934.
Photograph: Jack Pritchard Archive,
University of East Anglia.

MARS was another composite title invented by Wells Coates. It stood for the Modern Architectural Research Association, which was the British branch of the Congrès International d'Architecture Moderne (CIAM). Siegfried Giedion, the Swiss secretary of this group of avant-garde architects, had asked Wells to form a British branch in a letter of 28 February 1933. Architects such as Chermayeff, Maxwell Fry and the Tecton group were involved with Wells in MARS. Their first concern was with town planning, transport and social factors, rather than with individual buildings. Wells was able to attend the famous Athens Charter meeting of CIAM in July of that year as a British delegate, and there he met and talked with Le Corbusier and other leading architects. Giedion himself visited the MARS group in England, and he and Jack Pritchard first met at an early gathering of the group held at the Pritchards' house in Belsize Park Gardens in 1933.

The Lawn Road Flats, therefore, came at a time when both the architect and the client had arrived at similar ideas on how the problems of living in the modern city should be tackled, and after they had had time to absorb the lessons of the continental pioneers. Almost as soon as they were finished, in the summer of 1934, the international character of the Flats was increased by the influx of refugees from Hitler's Germany. Gropius and his wife arrived on 18 October and stayed at Lawn Road Flats until March 1937, when he was appointed Professor of Architecture at Harvard.[8] Marcel Breuer came in either the autumn of 1934 or the New Year of 1935, and stayed for a short while at the Flats before moving elsewhere. Moholy-Nagy arrived in May 1935 and also stayed for a few weeks at the Flats before he moved to Farm Walk, off the Finchley Road. Both Breuer and Moholy-Nagy also left England for America in 1937.

With the successful completion of the flats in Lawn Road, Isokon planned to put up similar blocks in Manchester and Birmingham, while the problem of housing families was to be tackled in the Sunspan houses and in larger flats with extensive amenities, in park land near Windsor. Gropius came over to work on the Manchester project with Maxwell Fry. He had visited England in May 1934 in connection with an exhibition of his work at the RIBA, and he had lectured to the DIA then. Morton Shand, with Jack Pritchard and Maxwell Fry, was responsible for inviting him over to work later that year.

Unfortunately, because of financial and other reasons, including public protest, none of the Isokon building schemes he was involved in came to anything. The scheme for St Leonard's Hill, Windsor, was the nearest to success. Royal permission was obtained and planning for this started in the winter of 1934, but Pritchard became ill and was unable to raise the large sum of money needed, and it was dropped in July of the following year. The scheme allowed for the preservation of the fine grounds of a ruined villa with magnificent trees overlooking Windsor Great Park itself. By building three blocks of flats rather than individual houses, the majority of the land and the views were to be retained for amenity use. Full facilities for eating, shopping, sport and the education of young children were also planned. Unfortunately, the exciting Isokon Sunspan model houses were also unbuilt, at least by Isokon. These were designed by Wells Coates according to Isokon principles, but in the spring of 1934 he sold the designs to a building firm called Berg. Berg displayed one of these houses at the Daily Mail Ideal Home Exhibition that year, with furniture by Gordon Russell Limited, and several were built.

The arrival in England of ex-Bauhaus masters of the calibre of Gropius, Breuer and Moholy-Nagy encouraged Pritchard to develop the idea of Isokon furniture. He discussed this with Gropius in October 1935 and Gropius agreed to become controller of design in the new Isokon Furniture Company, the formation of which was announced in the press in the New Year of 1936. Pritchard explained the company's policy in a contemporary memorandum which shows the influence of Gropius's thinking:

The general principle governing the policy will be in the designing, making and distributing of furniture, fittings and equipment which help to make contemporary living pleasanter, comfortable and more efficient . . . Uniformity

Breuer and Moholy-Nagy go to America.
Cartoon by Gordon Cullen, 1937.
Photograph: Jack Pritchard Archive,
University of East Anglia.

8   See David Elliot, *Gropius in England: a documentation 1934–37*, London, 1974, for more information on this period of Gropius's career.

ALPHABETICAL LIST OF GUESTS

A	Professor Abercrombie	6	
	Mrs. Patrick Abercrombie	106	
	Dr. Thomas Adams	127	
	Mrs. Mary Adams	67	
	Mr. E. W. Armstrong	84	
	Mrs. E. W. Armstrong	102	
	Mr. Ove Arup	25	
	Mrs. Ove Arup	124	
	Mr. D. Ascoli	109	
	Mr. Ray Atherton	133	
B	Mr. D. Betts	95	
	Mr. D. Betts's guest	96	
	Mr. Eric L. Bird	18	
	Mr. D. L. Bridgwater	93	
	Mrs. D. L. Bridgwater	22	
	Professor Lionel Budden	125	
C	Mr. William Cohn	94	
	Mr. Noel Carrington	123	
	Mr. Edward Carter	57	
	Mrs. Edward Carter	51	
	Mr. Cyril Carter	42	
	Mr. F. Charles	112	
	Mr. Serge Chermayeff	53	
	Mrs. Serge Chermayeff	28	
	Mr. Wells Coates	64	
	Mr. J. M. Cohen	62	
	Mrs. J. M. Cohen	65	
	Mr. Willard Connely	55	
	Professor W. G. Constable	105	
	Mr. George Cooke	59	
	Mrs. George Cooke	122	
	Mr. Graham Cunningham	97	
	Mrs. Graham Cunningham	119	
	Mrs. E. Curtis	117	
	Mr. D. Curtis	116	
D	Mrs. Hugh Dalton	32	
	Mr. W. Davies	121	
	Mr. Richard de la Mare	10	
	Miss Elizabeth Denby	128	
	Mr. T. Denman	103	
	Mrs. T. Denman	108	
	Mr. E. M. O'R. Dickey	129	
	Mrs. E. M. O'R. Dickey	54	
	Mr. J. G. F. Donaldson	74	
	Mrs. J. G. F. Donaldson	63	
F	Mr. Geoffrey Faber	4	
	Mr. Alexander Farquharson	77	
	Miss Ellen Frank	35	
F	Mr. Ernst L. Freud	46	
	Mrs. Ernst Freud	5	
	Mr. E. Maxwell Fry	83	
	Mrs. E. Maxwell Fry	88	
G	Dr. Siegfried Giedion	66	
	Mr. John Gloag	17	
	Mrs. John Gloag	78	
	Mr. V. H. Goldsmith	79	
	Mrs. Ise Gropius	1	
	Dr. Walter Gropius	135	
H	Mr. Val Harding	15	
	Mrs. Val Harding	58	
	Dr. R. Hargreaves	24	
	Mrs. Hargreaves	37	
	Mrs. Gillian Harrison	7	
	Mr. Ashley Havinden	39	
	Mrs. Ashley Havinden	82	
	Mr. G. Brian Herbert	111	
	Professor W. G. Holford	29	
	Mrs. W. G. Holford	9	
	Dr. Julian Huxley	●	
	Mrs. Julian Huxley	3	
I	Mr. Gilbert Inglefield	20	
	Mrs. Gilbert Inglefield	115	
J	Mr. R. T. James	92	
	Mrs. R. T. James	19	
K	Mr. H. Kallenbach	21	
	Mr. B. Katz	120	
	Mr. C. J. Kavanagh	101	
	Miss Gertrude Kolman	56	
L	Mr. R. S. Lambert	33	
	Miss Judith Ledeboer	80	
	Miss Jane Lidderdale	13	
M	Sir Ian MacAlister	31	
	Lady MacAlister	134	
	Mrs. Edward Maufe	43	
	Mr. J. E. R. McDonagh	34	
	Mrs. J. E. R. McDonagh	100	
	Mr. Charles Marriott	131	
	Mrs. Charles Marriott	30	
	Mr. Basil Marriott	99	
	Mrs. Hartley Mason	45	
	Mr. J. Duncan Miller	23	
M	Mrs. J. Duncan Miller	71	
	Professor L. Moholy-Nagy	72	
	Mrs. Moholy-Nagy	132	
	Mrs. Henry Moore	47	
	Mr. Henry Morris	70	
	Mr. H. G. Murphy	87	
N	Mr. Christopher Nicholson	38	
	Mr. Max Nicholson	12	
	Mr. Clifford Norton	14	
	Mrs. Clifford Norton	104	
P	Dr. N. Pevsner	61	
	Miss M. E. Pevsney	126	
	Dr. Arthur Upham Pope	16	
	Mr. Fleetwood C. Pritchard	89	
	Mrs. Fleetwood C. Pritchard	41	
	Mr. J. Craven Pritchard	36	
	Mrs. J. Craven Pritchard	69	
Q	Mr. Hugh Quigley	90	
R	Dr. M. Rachlis	86	
	Mr. A. B. Read	40	
	Mr. Herbert Read	68	
	Professor C. H. Reilly	44	
	Mr. Paul Reilly	60	
	Mr. J. M. Richards	11	
	Mr. Michael Ross	50	
	Mr. Gordon Russell	52	
S	Mr. Godfrey Samuel	48	
	Mr. P. Morton Shand	8	
	Mrs. P. Morton Shand	26	
	Dr. S. Sieghein	76	
	Mr. J. Dixon Spain	118	
	Mr. C. D. Spragg	98	
	Mrs. Cunninghame Strettle	110	
	Mr. John Summerson	27	
	Mr. Cyril Sweett	113	
	Mrs. Cyril Sweett	91	
V	Mr. R. Vaughan	114	
	Mrs. Dorothea Ventris	75	
W	Mr. C. H. Waddington	49	
	Mrs. C. H. Waddington	73	
	Sir Alexander Walker	107	
	Lady Walston	130	
	Mr. Richard Weininger	85	
	Mr. H. G. Wells	2	
	Mr. Clough Williams-Ellis	81	

Cover of menu for Walter Gropius's leaving dinner. Jack Pritchard Archive, University of East Anglia.

Seating list for Walter Gropius's leaving dinner, 9 March 1937. Jack Pritchard Archive, University of East Anglia.

in character and design, combined with variety and individuality of each item should be achieved . . . In order to achieve variety and liveliness in design, while at the same time maintaining continuity of purpose, Professor Walter Gropius has agreed to act as consultant and will be the arbiter. This does not mean that he will not design himself, on the contrary it is hoped that he will have time to make considerable contributions of original work. Other designers working for the company will work in harmony with him and under his instructions. A scheme whereby young designers can gain experience in a practical business with the possibility of doing original work is to be worked out, for while outside designers will be employed it will be necessary to maintain a small staff who can carry out progressive and continuous research into design. The principal material to be used in the preliminary work must be plywood, taking full advantage of the possibilities of moulded plywood, whether in panel form or otherwise. Metal may be incorporated just where it performs a function better than plywood . . . The furniture will be primarily useful and its aesthetic qualities will be due to its form rather than superimposed ornament . . . In chairs, comfort will be the objective. Much recent modern furniture has failed to give the traditional English comfort tho' its form and shape has been pleasing . . . The old idea that good furniture should be heavy is fallacious, light plywood construction in aeroplanes has taught us a great many lessons. And how much easier it is to have furniture that is absolutely rigid but can also be moved about with utmost ease. We have all suffered from heavy immovable furniture.[9]

By this date, Pritchard had already had considerable experience in the design and production of modern furniture, using new

9 Pritchard archive.

techniques and materials. He had designed a cabinet in metal-faced plywood, a cantilever metal tube and plywood chair, and a desk in blockboard. At the time of the formation of Isokon and the planning for the Lawn Road Flats in c.1932–3, Wells Coates had designed some plywood storage units for the firm and he had equipped the Minimum Flat at the Dorland Hall Exhibition with very advanced furniture. Isokon also sold practical and well-designed plywood furniture from other firms, such as the light-weight stool which came from Venesta and the trolley which they took over from Makers of Simple Furniture. Some ten days before Gropius arrived to work in this country, Pritchard had visited a furniture firm in Zurich called Wohnbedarf, to which Siegfried Giedion introduced him, to buy a selection of metal furniture by Breuer, Aalto and other pioneer designers. In the autumn of 1934 and the following New Year, there were plans, from which little came, for Isokon to produce and sell Wohnbedarf metal furniture in England under licence. An exhibition of Aalto's plywood furniture, organised by the *Architectural Review* at Fortnum & Masons in the winter of 1933, seems to have opened the eyes of many designers in England to the potentialities of laminated wood construction, and Aalto may well have been an important influence on Pritchard when he set up his firm. In August 1935 he made a brief visit to Finland with Morton Shand and Graham Reid, a director of Venesta, and Aalto showed

Walter Gropius, Occasional Table, c.1936.
Birch plywood, rexine.
University of East Anglia Collection.
Photograph: Michael Brandon-Jones.

them his Paimio sanatorium. On this trip, Pritchard also saw the workshops where Aalto's Finmar furniture was made. The first Isokon furniture to use bent, pre-formed laminated wood with no metal parts seems to have been the chairs and tables designed by Marcel Breuer in 1936.

When the Isokon Furniture Company was set up in the winter of 1935, Jack Pritchard left Venesta, who retained him as a consultant for two or three years, to concentrate on his own firm. Gropius and Breuer were called in and most of the famous examples of Isokon furniture were designed in 1936 – the Long Chair and the nesting tables date from this year. Breuer designed both of these and, on the whole, his designs were more successful than those of Gropius. Neither of them seems to have used plywood much before this, although Breuer did design a cot and some nursery furniture in this material while at the Bauhaus. Plywood, unlike metal, is pleasant to touch. Its lightness also makes it suitable for use in furniture which is frequently moved about, such as stacking chairs and nesting tables, while its resilience means that the chairs are springy and that

Marcel Breuer, Isokon Long Chair, 1936.
Laminated birch frame and
upholstered plywood seat.
University of East Anglia Collection.
Photograph: Michael Brandon-Jones.

Gerald Summers, chair for Makers of
Simple Furniture, 1933–4. Birch plywood.
University of East Anglia Collection.
Photograph: Michael Brandon-Jones.

the tables can be placed on uneven surfaces without rocking. The
curves in the plywood construction give Breuer's Isokon furniture
an organic character which is markedly different from his tense,
rectilinear Bauhaus designs. It is worth noting that the paintings
and constructions made by Moholy-Nagy in England have similar
bent, organic forms which also strongly differ from the simpler
geometric ones of his Bauhaus period. A contemporary critic, Clive
Entwistle, engagingly remarked that Breuer's Isokon furniture had
'an economy of line and form comparable with that of a leopard or
an orchid'.[10]

The startling originality of the Isokon furniture presented Pritchard
with problems in marketing it. To explain its eminent practicality
and its comfort he had a series of sales leaflets produced, some
designed by Moholy-Nagy. These leaflets are remarkable for their
clarity and they have helped to spread the 'Isokon Idea' amongst
avant-garde architects and the intelligentsia, who were the main
clients for the furniture. Outlets were also found with some leading
furniture stores: Dunn's of Bromley (probably the first), Crofton
Gane's of Bristol, Heal's, Bowman's and John Lewis in London. In
1937, Pritchard persuaded John Lewis to set up a stand designed by
Gropius to display modern furniture, not only from Isokon but from
Finmar, the firm which distributed Aalto's furniture, and from
Thonet and other leading firms. The selection was made by John
Gloag, Marcel Breuer and Professor C H Reilly. Pritchard also
displayed his furniture at the Ideal Home Exhibition in 1937 and at

Marcel Breuer, Isokon dining table
and four chairs, 1936. Plywood.
University of East Anglia Collection.
Photograph: Michael Brandon-Jones.

[10] C Entwistle, 'An Approach to Interior Design',
Architectural Review, December 1937, p.226.

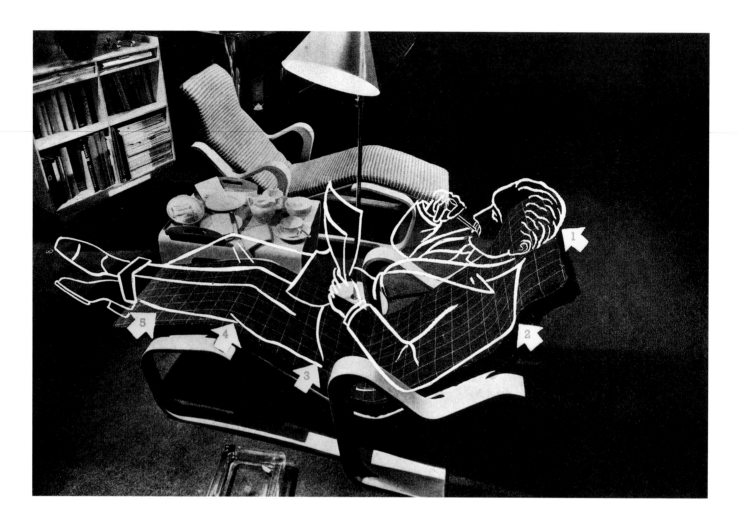

Moholy Nagy's original advertisement
for the Isokon Long Chair.
Jack Pritchard Archive,
University of East Anglia.

a MARS Group exhibition at the New Burlington Galleries in January 1938. Sales during these early years were not great, but the ground was 'prepared for future expansion which was sadly cut off by the outbreak of the war'. In a letter of 22 June 1938, Pritchard seems to have been quite pleased to inform Breuer, who had gone to America, that Isokon was then producing eight or nine Long Chairs a week.

Breuer had become controller of design at Isokon after Gropius left in March 1937, but he had gone to America in July that year – partly to investigate the American market for Isokon products – and had decided to settle down there by September. Before he left, he had designed a club with dining facilities on the ground floor of the Lawn Road Flats. This club, the Isobar, was opened early in November 1937. It was furnished with Isokon furniture, a wide variety of journals were taken, and well-cooked and economically-priced meals could be eaten there by members and their guests. With Philip Harben as manager and members as discriminating as Raymond Postgate, the gastronomic standard of the club was high, and it provided an ideal social centre for the area. As the Flats were built of reinforced concrete, it also served in the war years as a shelter during air-raids and some members would sleep there after an evening's entertainment.

The **ISOKON LONG CHAIR** gives scientific relaxation to every part of the body, immediately creating a feeling of well-being. It is even a better aid to digestion than any medicine under the sun. Admirable for those who take forty winks after dinner.

Before he left, Breuer also reworked several old designs for aluminium furniture to be produced by Isokon, but these do not seem to have got beyond the prototype stage. Sometime after Breuer's departure, Pritchard felt the need for a professional designer's advice, and in the spring of 1939, Arthur Korn, who succeeded Breuer as partner to F R S Yorke, came in to help direct the firm. In the same year, another refugee, Egon Riss, who lived in the Flats, designed in collaboration with Pritchard a group of interesting examples of plywood furniture for Isokon. Among this group are the Gull, the Bottleship, the Pocket Bottleship and the Isokon Penguin Donkey. These are even more organic in character than Breuer's furniture, for they are made of very thin plywood formed into pronounced curves. Their continuous flowing lines resemble those found in Naum Gabo's contemporary sculpture and, as Pritchard was in contact with Gabo at this time, the resemblance is not perhaps fortuitous. Unfortunately, these pieces again hardly got beyond the prototype stage before the outbreak of the war.

The war cut off the supply of plywood parts from Finland and Estonia, and the Isokon Furniture Company had to cease production. There were attempts to revive it towards the end of the war as a Utility Furniture Company, but these came to nothing. Another

Wells Coates, Embassy Court, Brighton, 1934.
Photograph: British Architectural Library,
RIBA, London.

scheme for Geoffrey Dunn of Dunn's of Bromley to take it over also failed. In 1949, Jack Pritchard became director of the Furniture Development Council and it was only after his retirement in 1963 that he was able to revive the Isokon Furniture Company. Breuer's Long Chair and nesting tables were produced again, the former in a slightly modified design by Breuer himself, which made the lower end of the seat wider than before, As the thin plywood used to make the Bottleship and the Penguin Donkey was no longer made, Pritchard commissioned Ernest Race to produce new designs.

The Lawn Road Flats survived the war despite a near-miss from a bomb on 9 September 1940, which blew in the windows. Although the fabric was sound, the Flats had weathered badly and in 1955 they were treated with a white pebble-textured stucco. Originally a cream-coloured paint had been applied direct to the concrete. The Flats were sold to the *New Statesman* in January 1969 and then, early in 1972, to the Camden Council. Sadly, the Isobar was closed down and converted into flats by the *New Statesman*. It had never been a profit-making venture, but with its disappearance the sense of community which had been such an important part of life in the Lawn Road Flats also vanished.

Marcel Breuer, Isokon Dining Table, 1936.
Bentwood. Design Museum.

This article was originally written for the catalogue which accompanied the exhibition, *Hampstead in the Thirties*, Camden Art Centre, London, 1974, and is reproduced by kind permission of the author.

London Transport Design

JEREMY REWSE-DAVIES

The Early Years

The Roundel, the Johnston typeface, the Beck underground map, the Holden stations, the posters and the Routemaster bus. To have provided one of these would be a source of pride for any company, but for one company to be responsible for so many design icons is a truly remarkable achievement. That London Transport has a reputation for good, co-ordinated design is undeniable; why this should be so is a rather curious story. How did an habitually under-funded transport undertaking acquire a reputation for design and the management of design that has lasted over half a century – a reputation that is so implanted into the company's culture that even now the extension to one of its lines should be the occasion for a celebration of architectural excellence?

The story starts in the early years of the century with the appointment of a man called Frank Pick to run the publicity office of the Underground Group. Pick had previously worked in the office of the managing director but had been constantly critical of the company's posters and publicity. His interest was rewarded with the responsibility for improving things. At this stage nothing in Pick's early life and career had indicated an interest in visual things. He was born the son of a Lincolnshire draper in 1878, collected a degree in law in 1902, and went to work first for GNER and then followed his boss, Sir George Gibb, to the Underground Group in 1906.

The Underground Group's publicity at this time was uninspiring, relying almost entirely on long, written descriptions and lists of destinations. Pick quickly changed the approach, creating punchy illustrated posters quite unlike anything produced by the Group's competitors. However this was only the beginning. He saw very quickly that to be successful the product had to match the publicity. The immediate objects of his attentions were posters, which by

Frank Pick, 1939.
Photograph: London Transport Museum.

covering the available wall space in haphazard fashion served to confuse the passenger and degrade the environment. Pick pleaded for fewer, better-quality advertisements combined with clearer station names and signing. He was allowed to experiment with this 'new way' provided income did not fall. In the event, revenue from advertising improved and Pick received many letters from passengers praising the clarity of the revamped platforms.

He had also become dissatisfied with the lettering used to display the company's name and its services, and commissioned Edward Johnston to design a new typeface. Although Johnston, a man who distrusted commerce in all its forms, was a curious choice, the result was a typeface of purity and clarity that has survived in updated form until the present day.

Charles Holden, Station Mock-up, Earl's Court, 1926. Photograph: London Transport Museum.

The posters meanwhile had improved as Pick took a greater interest in the artists and employed younger ones, such as the American Edward McKnight Kauffer. Although he had certainly became interested in art, this was never as an isolated activity. He saw the posters as a strictly commercial enterprise whose job was to increase revenue for the company; a partnership of art and industry.

As his interest in design grew, he became involved in the Design and Industries Association (DIA) and through it met some of the biggest influences in his life, particularly designer Harold Stabler, and later the architect Charles Holden. He became chairman of the DIA in 1921, but his commercial interests kept pace, and in the same year he became joint assistant managing director of the Underground Group, an arrangement that lasted for three years before Pick took over both halves of the job.

Pre-1930 Morden extension

His work with the DIA and his expanded area of influence at work kindled an interest in architecture and in creating a new architectural idiom for the Underground. He was convinced that the key to attracting passengers to go underground was to allow light into as much of the area of a station as possible, and hated the mean, dark entrances of most stations. His view was that 'the station was a shop in which you received the customer', an idea many years ahead of contemporary thinking. A contact he had made in the DIA was Charles Holden, an architect who had previously worked in the style of the Arts and Crafts Movement, but who was seeking an opportunity to be more adventurous. Holden was employed first on a back entrance to Westminster which was considered satisfactory, and then, with the passing of the Bill to allow the extension to the City and South London line, Holden was given a larger canvas. The test for the 'new idiom' was the second batch of stations. Most of these

Charles Holden, Sudbury Town Station, 1931.
Photograph: London Transport Museum.

were corner sites, but no two were alike, so if there were to be a standard solution it would have to be designed to allow for flexibility.

Holden's response was to design a series of folding screen facades in Portland stone, an ingenious device that allowed the angles to be changed to suit the site. The folding screen device was tested with a full-size mock-up in a workshop in Earls Court. The entrance was double height with a glazed front allowing light to flood into the ticket hall and to back illuminate the large company logo at night. The logo was something else Pick had had a hand in. Writing at the time, Pick was clearly excited by the possibilities of the new style:

By way of an exciting finish, I may say that we are going to build our stations upon the Morden extension railway to the most modern pattern. We are going to discard entirely all ornament. We are going to build in reinforced concrete. The station will be simply a hole in the wall, everything being sacrificed to the doorway and some notice above to tell you to what the doorway leads. We are

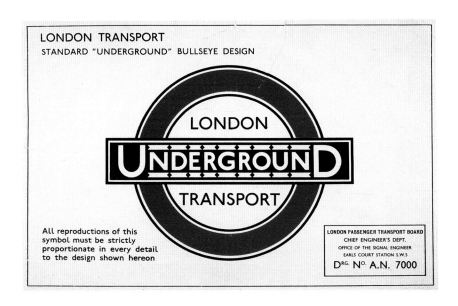

Roundel showing standard 'bull's-eye' design.
Photograph: London Transport Museum.

going to represent the DIA gone mad, and in order that I may go mad in good company I have got Holden to see that we do it properly.

In his excitement about the architecture he didn't forget other elements, and at the same time wrote to Holden about posters:

There is one matter which, one day, will come up for solution, the exhibition of posters upon the outside, and while it is not the intention to put posters upon the outside of this station at this time, we should have in mind that some day they will appear. It seems to me that there is space for posters upon the piers, and it will be wise that you should consider this problem now rather than that it should be patched later.

St John's Wood Road Station, 1933.
Photograph: London Transport Museum.

The posters by now were attracting a great deal of attention. Many of the artists commissioned were influenced by the European art movements and the Underground became a gallery of populist interpretation of movements such as Cubism, Futurism and Vorticism. By now it was clear that the Underground was successfully using design in the furtherance of its business.

1930 Piccadilly extension

All this had whetted Pick's appetite for his new idiom so that when the extension to the Piccadilly line was agreed in 1930, he saw it as an opportunity to improve on what had gone before. It occurred to Pick that with such an opportunity to do something really new, he and Holden should explore what was being done elsewhere, and so, in July 1930, they set out on a journey around northern Europe. For two and a half weeks they inspected public buildings in Berlin, Hamburg, and Cologne; they also went to Holland, Denmark and Sweden. Both were impressed by the simple unpretentiousness of much that they saw, but were also critical.

Opposite page:
Edward McKnight Kauffer, *London Museum,*
1922. Poster for London Transport.
London Transport Museum

LONDON HISTORY AT THE

LONDON MUSEUM

DOVER STREET
OR ST. JAMES'S PARK STATION.

Everywhere in Sweden you see experiment taking place, but experiment which is not wholly successful. It almost always reflects something else which can be seen to better advantage in some other city of the world . . . The elements of failure appear in all sorts of places. It is no doubt extraordinary that there should be so much experiment taking place in a relatively small place like Stockholm, but the accomplishment is not such as to warrant Stockholm being held up to us as an example.

Elsewhere, although there were interesting new stations such as Olympia station and Krumme Lanke in Germany, there was no attempt to achieve consistency across a system or part of a system.

What had really impressed Pick were the simple brick buildings of Hilversum and Bussum in Holland. In his report to the Board he talks of their successful blend of tradition with modern values through the continuing use of brick; he also commends their sanity and highly-developed civic sense. This last is an important point, for although Pick was that rare combination – an enthusiast for design and an efficient commercial manager – at the heart of everything he did was a belief that design must add value to society. Objects must be fit for purpose but each must be better than the last, expressing something of the civilisation in which it was created and enabling man to improve his lot. 'Labour is not civilisation unless it leads to leisure, and wealth without art is barbarism.' Translating these principles into London's transport undertaking meant that he believed that by using the best design and architecture it was a civilising influence on the capital.

Returning to the task of designing the stations of the Piccadilly Line, he tried to put into action the ideas he had seen in Europe, particularly at William Dudok's Hilversum Town Hall. Functionalism based on the necessities of construction and plan, fulfilling its task of eliminating all that was superfluous and extraneous. In essence, the principle of Modernism, and yet Dudok's Town Hall was not within the mainstream of Modernism, either in its modest appear-ance or in its use of materials, but it was here that Pick found what he had been looking for.

The first new station of the extension was at Sudbury Town, a simple, well-detailed, unpretentious brick box with a flat roof and tall glazed openings running the full height of the building. The interior was equally plain and was arranged to promote the most efficient movement of people, but here Pick's interests in content as well as building were allowed full rein. Pick had felt that a good building was in itself not enough – every element that the passenger saw or used should be treated with equal care to create a harmonious whole. This feeling had been increased by what he saw in Denmark: not exceptional buildings or objects but the consistent use of good designers to address every aspect of a job, however small.

Leicester Square Station, 1935.
Photograph: London Transport Museum.

The beginnings of design management

In the summer of 1930, Pick sent a memorandum addressed both to the general manager and the chief civil engineer, instructing them to supply Holden with a complete specification of all the equipment required for each of the stations along the line. 'Nothing shall be built,' he said, 'which has not been specifically designed to conform with the general architectural scheme.' This was something quite new for the Underground, and indeed it was perhaps the first time in any major company that 'co-ordinated design' across all elements was attempted or even thought possible. With hindsight we can see here the beginnings of an attempt to 'manage' design across a broad spectrum.

Bussum Railway Station, Holland.
Photograph: London Transport Museum.

This first attempt was not entirely successful, and what he wrote at the time will find echoes among many design managers today:

On the platforms I found that some seven or eight automatic machines have been dumped down and are now going to spoil the cleanness and clearness of the platforms. Somehow there seems to be a desire on the part of everyone to break up and destroy the tidiness and spaciousness of this station. The only way in which, in my opinion, the spaciousness can be filled properly is by passengers, and not by a lot of impediments . . . Going over the bridge I note that the whole of the lighting of the bridge is an afterthought. The bulkhead lights are now being screwed on to the concrete instead of being sunk into the concrete as would have been done if the lighting had been designed properly and at the proper time. There is an entire lack of design and orderly workmanship.

He continued in the same vein when considering the next stations in the programme:

Unless some special effort is made, there is every prospect that the stations and works will have to be botched, just as Sudbury Town station had to be botched, by a failure to have a clear plan of what is required before the work is carried out. I think, therefore, we should have placed before us, at once, plans showing the lighting scheme for all stations, and the whole of the miscellaneous equipment required; also plans showing the location and form of all signs and notices at stations, and a plan showing the water supply and any further arrangements that may be necessary for cleaning. We cannot regard a station as being approved for execution until all these various plans are agreed.

From this dissatisfaction about the process came the notion that he must control all design aspects of a job, and the concept of managed design was embedded in the procedures.

During the next few years, in partnership with Holden, he remorselessly put these principles into practice, sometimes with conspicuous success such as Southgate and Arnos Grove, stations that Hugh Casson later called 'perfect examples of functionalism' and Ian Nairn, writing 30 years later, described as the first modern

Charles Holden, Arnos Grove Station, 1932.
Photograph: London Transport Museum.

buildings in England which did not throw their style in the public's face. This comment perhaps holds the key to their success in importing uncompromisingly modern buildings into suburban environments.

1933 London Transport

In June 1933, London Transport came into existence – brought about in Herbert Morrison's words 'to eliminate wasteful competition'. The new organisation covered the Underground Group, plus buses and trams. Pick was to be chief executive and deputy chairman. His task was herculean; he was to take over responsibility for five railway companies, 17 tramways, 66 bus companies and part of 69 other bus or coach companies. To make matters worse each deal was done separately and the conditions

Trainee bus conductors, 1935.
Photograph: London Transport Museum.

varied from company to company. Clearly integrating all these disparate groups into one homogenous whole was never going to be easy, but somehow it was achieved, and here again Pick used the power of design to help him achieve his aims.

LT terrazzo-finish bus stop, 1937.
Photograph: London Transport Museum.

The accompanying illustration tells the whole story. Pick realised that, as with an army, if you take recruits from different backgrounds with different loyalties, you must first strip away all evidence of a former life, dress your recruits the same, pay them the same and treat them the same to create a new loyalty. There are few such examples of the power of corporate identity to help create one company from a multiplicity of others.

Almost unbelievably, whilst all this was going on, Pick had accepted the role of chairman of the New Council for Art and Industry. That

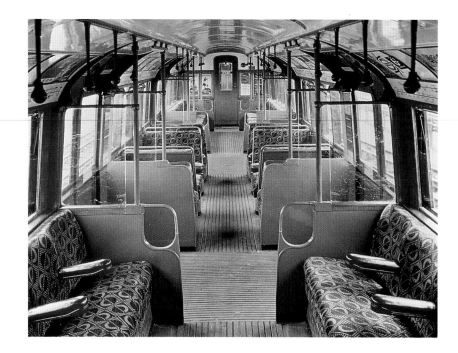

Underground train stock interior, 1938.
Photograph: London Transport Museum.

Shannon Corner, Malden, 1933.
Photograph: London Transport Museum.

his name was the first choice shows how successfully he straddled the worlds of design and industry.

The work at London Transport continued as it had in the Underground Group. Buses, bus shelters, trolley buses and trams were given the same attention as stations and publicity had been given in the past. An example of this is the bus stop. Buses were no longer allowed to stop on a casual basis, and a large number of fixed bus stops signs had appeared on the street – mostly of dubious quality, adding nothing to the cityscape. Pick immediately saw two opportunities: to use bus stops as a signal of LT services and responsibilities, and to provide street furniture that made a positive impact on the city's streets. The simple concrete post and enamel flag introduced in 1937 was so successful that it remained virtually unchanged for 50 years. His one admitted failure was to come to terms with the overhead wires required by the trolley bus – the replacement for trams. Although he wrote that the arrangement should be logical and geometric, he was never happy with the results.

The design of the vehicles was included in the co-ordinated image. Trams and buses, too, were developed that added to the pleasure of the journey, and within vehicles, the designs of the moquettes on the seats gave him and, one hopes, the passengers, as much pleasure as the design of the vehicles themselves.

Nothing was forgotten or ignored; everything was 'fit for purpose'.

The legacy

Sir Nicholas Pevsner, writing soon after Pick's death, described London Transport as 'the most efficacious centre of visual education in England'. Pick would have liked that phrase as he always believed that harnessing art and design to the business aims of a public enterprise was not only worthwhile, but essential in order that both might benefit.

His use of the best artists and industrial designers of the day to design what had hitherto been considered mundane and unimportant; his determination to find a new architectural idiom based on the modern style, but one in which the purposes of the enterprise were as important as the architect: all this made him perhaps the most important influence on architecture and design in the first half of the century.

London Transport has continued to believe in design and to use design well, nearly always employing the best designers and architects to manage or create designs for the system. One thinks of

Paul Nash, *Come in to Play / Come out to Live*, 1936. Posters for London Transport. Paul & Karen Rennie Collection.

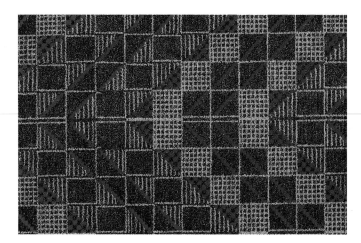

Enid Marx, *Chevron*, c.1935. Woollen moquette
for underground train seating.
London Transport Museum.

Marion Dorn, *Leaf*, c.1937. Woollen moquette
for underground train seating.
London Transport Museum.

Misha Black's work on the Victoria Line, the Routemaster bus with
work by Douglas Scott, and buildings such as Stockwell bus garage
and the more successful decorated stations such as Charing Cross by
David Gentleman, and yet – perhaps with the exception of the
Victoria Line – the designs were 'one offs', lacking the guiding hand
of a man totally committed to the combination of art and industry,
and the service of the community.

At a talk he gave to students of the Royal College of Art, Pick said:
'Our civilisation for a century or more has been pursuing wealth,
knowledge, mastery over nature, mastery over man. Everywhere
there is an endeavour after order, grace, beauty. What is needed is
someone to sort out the pieces and turn the jigsaw puzzle into something whole and plain.'

He need not have looked any further than at himself to fulfil the
role.

Paul Nash as Designer

ANDREW CAUSEY

No other leading English artist in the 1930s was so involved with design as Paul Nash.[1] Nash's design work was primarily graphic and flat pattern, for posters, book jackets and textiles, but it extended to glass, china, and interior design.

It was not unusual for English artists to be involved in design work in the 1930s, but Nash's range of activities was untypically wide. He helped to open up debate about the role of the artist in industry, promoting English design through contributions to journals, particularly the *Architectural Review* and *The Listener*, and his collection of essays on design, *Room and Book* (1932), was reviewed in at least 20 journals and papers.[2] Nash took public initiatives on behalf of the design community, through membership of the Society of Industrial Artists (1930) and his presidency of the Society (1932–4), as well as membership of the Board of Trade's Council for Art and Industry, established in the wake of the Gorell Report on the relationship of art to industry (1932). Nash did two short spells of part-time teaching in the design school at the Royal College of Art (1924–5 and 1938–40), and was one of two artists appointed to the committee set up to bring the College in closer touch with the needs of industry.

Nash put his weight behind exhibitions, partly – it is true – to promote his own work. In 1931 he organised his work on books (bindings, jackets, illustrations) into a show at the art gallery run by Batsford, the publishers. He had a close relationship with Zwemmer's, the art bookshop, and in 1932, to coincide with the publication of *Room and Book*, organised a show of contemporary art and design work at the adjoining Zwemmer Gallery, including out-and-out Modernists like Serge Chermayeff, and hand-block textile design artists he particularly admired: Phyllis Barron, Dorothy Larcher and Marion Dorn. Later, in 1943, Nash had a retrospective exhibition of his own design work by the Council for Encouragement of Music and the Arts (predecessor of the Arts

Notes

[1] Basic research on Nash as a designer was undertaken by Anthony Bertram for his *Paul Nash: the portrait of an artist*, London, 1955. The most important source of information is the catalogue by Susan Lambert for the Victoria and Albert Museum's 1975 exhibition, *Paul Nash as Designer*.

[2] Nash's press cuttings books are in the National Art Library at the Victoria and Albert Museum.

Oliver Hill, Midland Hotel, Morecambe, 1930,
showing dining room with rug
designed by Marion Dorn.
Photograph: Architectural Press.

Council) at the gallery attached to its offices in Belgrave Square.
In his catalogue introduction, Nash wrote of the 'development and
change of view taking place over a number of years in the practice
of applied design alongside the practice of painting . . . The two
occupations, picture making and applied design, as expressed in
relation to printed and woven textiles and in decorations for books
and so on, do not work eccentrically but in close sympathy. Although the latter occupation is often regarded as a "side line" it
cannot be regarded as a branch line but rather an integral part of
the main system . . .'

That could be said by someone looking back over their work in the
1930s, when non-figurative art was a serious issue for Nash, and coming to terms with the abstracting, conventionalising needs of poster
and textile design work could be seen as complementary. In truth,
though, Nash was first and foremost a painter, and there were other
moments in his career when art and design work were less obviously
complementary. His gradual withdrawal from design work from the
mid-1930s has been connected with his poor health and lack of time
and energy. Without denying that, one can add that Surrealism and
the flights of the imagination reflected in his late work made the
intricacies of small pattern abstract designs for Underground train
seats seem less relevant.

Different impulses and events lay behind Nash's 1930s design work. One was his experiment with abstraction in painting, which was supported by his textile and pattern paper designs. A second was the Depression, which left the art market enfeebled and artists casting around for other sources of income. Thirdly, the role of the artist in industry became a public issue, with the government's sudden and belated recognition that good design helped trade in manufactures and that Britain had paid less heed to this, in the course of the century, than its commercial rivals. Nash's design work, his design writing and journalism, and his practical efforts on behalf of British design, were concentrated into the first half of the 1930s. By late 1933, when the arrival in England of Walter Gropius signalled the start of the influx of distinguished modernist artists, architects and designers, in flight from fascism, Nash's contribution was already slowing down. His role was in helping British design bridge the gap between the 1920s and the new decade, and contributing to the early stages of the new movement. It was a moment with its own particular character, when Modernism in terms of new materials as well as forms was spreading rapidly in England, but within an aesthetic context in which the Arts and Crafts Movement was still strong.

For ten years after 1919, England had lacked an avant-garde in visual culture. It was essentially a 'neo-Georgian' decade, largely country-based and landscape inspired. There was minimal knowledge of either the Bauhaus or De Stijl, and none at all of Russian Constructivism. As a result, there was little understanding in the English design community in the 1920s of the postwar European social idealism, the idea that design could offer a moral as well as a practical lead towards the creation of a better society. It was only with Herbert Read's *Art and Industry* in 1934, and the proselytising of Gropius and others for Bauhaus ideals, that the ethos began to establish itself in England. There had been hints of new commitment earlier. The fitting out of the new Broadcasting House for the BBC between 1930 and 1934 by Serge Chermayeff, Raymond McGrath and Wells Coates, was exceptional – the reflection of the idea that a new kind of public service accompanied by new technology required a reformed design approach. Nash's situation was different from that of the younger men. Half a generation older than those three, Nash was English (though McGrath and Coates came from Commonwealth countries and were English speakers, all the above were foreign-born), and his work was rooted in established English traditions. Although Nash expressed no reservations about the most innovative modern work in his writings on contemporary design and in the administrative support for it, there was, nonetheless, a difference between the traditions he envisaged Modernism fitting into, which he saw as national, and the Corbusian concept followed by the BBC's designers, which was associated with rationalism and fitness for purpose, and was, in essence, inter-

Wells Coates, AD 65 radio for Ekco, 1934.
Design Museum.

national. While Nash looked back to the precepts of the English eighteenth century and the Regency, which, at its highest point of development, he regarded as a culture that had been destroyed by Victorian eclecticism and excess, the Corbusian standard was an architectural type-form, the Parthenon, which Corbusier could regard as beyond any national tradition. Until the mid-1930s, the universal sense of urgent need to improve the quality of British design and embed Modernism concealed these different viewpoints. As the process of embedding succeeded, divergences became obvious. In 1935, Nash used the phrase 'for, but not with'[3] to describe the significance that non-figurative art had had for him, and his unreserved support for innovation and experiment, but his discovery at the same time that, in the end, he did not altogether go along with it personally.

Nash was taking much greater risks in his painting in the early 1930s than he had dared in the slightly staid atmosphere of the previous decade, and saw architects and designers doing the same. He felt, in the development of abstraction, a new affinity with Modernist architects and designers, but also saw that in other areas of Modernist activity, groups were forming in order to maximise effective strength. Nash had long advocated professional interest groups,[4] and in 1933, planning the avant-garde artists' and architects' group, Unit One, he was drawn to Wells Coates as an ally and participant, partly because of Coates's success in setting up the Modern Architectural Research Group earlier that year, as the British wing of the Congrès Internationaux d'Architecture Moderne (CIAM). There was a sense of new, collective beginnings. Early in 1932, for example, Frank Pick took over the presidency of the Design and Industries Association (DIA) from Clough Williams Ellis, with the aim of making it a central force in design, immediately establishing sub-groups to look at the design of specific types of manufacture. It was part of Nash's contribution to enter this new arena of collective action on behalf of the community of experimental artists. Nash's seriousness about new design led him to membership of the Society of Industrial Artists (SIA), founded by Milner Gray and others in 1930. The SIA was smaller than the DIA and less influential, but, unlike the DIA, looked after the interests, specifically, of artists working as industrial designers. When Nash was president, the council included architects like Serge Chermayeff, and designers such as Denham MacLaren, whose steel and glass furniture Nash had singled out for praise in 1930,[5] but also the sculptor, Frank Dobson, and the painter, Graham Sutherland. It was the shape of organisation that Nash liked and wanted.

In 1930 Nash had written that 'in order to encourage the production of good modern work, some system of centralisation is obviously necessary. London should have at least one centre where all the best examples of modern production could be obtained. This centre should either be equipped with its own staff of designers and craftsmen, or control the independent worker, to the extent of being able to rely on his efficient co-operation. An organisation of this kind could command the best workers in every medium, and its establishment would be the incentive so much needed towards experiment and study.'[6] Although Nash was not, by 1930, the only person expressing these sentiments, he needs to be credited with articulating here the core conclusion of the Gorell Report of 1932. The Gorell Committee had been established the previous year by the Board of Trade to examine the role of the artist in industry and the marketing of design manufactures. It was the government's response to the decline in competitiveness of British manufactures, and to the disastrous fall in industrial output caused by the Depression. Gorell recommended a centre in London to carry out the function the Tate Gallery fulfilled for modern art.[7] Though Nash was not on the Gorell Committee, whose only painter member was Roger Fry, he sat on the Board of Trade's follow-up committee, the Council for Art and Industry, chaired by Frank Pick. This committee extended Gorell's remit and reported on deepening consumer understanding of design, as well as improving designers' relations with manufacturers. The 1937 report of the Council for Art and Industry, which Nash as a committee member joined in signing, listed as one of its three main aims the overcoming of mutual distrust between artists and manufacturers.[8] This was the issue that preoccupied Nash most of all, and the influence of his ideas is seriously felt in the report.

[3] Paul Nash, 'For, but not With', *Axis*, 1, January 1935.

[4] For an early example of Nash's arguing for strength through forming groups, see Paul Nash 'Gilman and the Groups', *New Witness*, 25 April 1919.

[5] Paul Nash, 'Modern English Furnishing', *Architectural Review*, January 1930.

[6] *Ibid.*

[7] *Art and Industry. Report of the Committee appointed by the Board of Trade under the Chairmanship of Lord Gorell on the Production and Exhibition of Articles of Good Design and Every-day Use*, London, 1932, p.42.

[8] *Design and the Designer in Industry. Report of the Council for Art and Industry*, London, 1937.

Apart from bookplates, book illustration and occasional posters, Nash's achievement in design by 1930 was in the areas of textile and end- or pattern-paper design. His involvement with both started through his friend, Claud Lovat Fraser, a pioneer, after the First World War, of the revival of seventeenth- and eighteenth-century small pattern designs. Gordon Craig had given Lovat Fraser a Florentine daybook bound in a traditional pattern paper, and triggered an interest in pattern-papers that Lovat Fraser passed on to Nash. Nash's subsequent visit to see the Rizzi pattern-paper collection in the Victoria and Albert Museum led him, in 1927, to write in an article on the papers: 'It is always a relief to be rid of the responsibility of representation. To concern oneself solely with the problem of formal relationships is to escape into a new world. Here one is in touch with pure reality, and the business of make-believe gives place to other considerations in many ways far more satisfying.'[9]

Though Nash never directly equated abstraction in painting and pattern design, the two fed into one another in this key period of the late 1920s and early 1930s. In the first article on Nash as a designer,[10] in 1928, Darcy Braddell described how, in his textile designs, Nash was preoccupied with the subordination of ornament in modern rooms and the need for textile designers, however abstract their designs might be, to compensate for this through the implication of shallow space in the design. Braddell took the example of Abstract No. 3, which foreshadows designs for paintings based on wooden scaffolds for advertisement hoarding that Nash started only the following year, 1929. Nash believed that the plainness of modern architecture required, in ancillary areas such as curtain and carpet design, a degree of visual complexity and controlled depth of design in order to arrest and interest the eye and to relieve the bareness of the architecture, but that interest had to be created without a collapse into ornamentation, decor, or excess. The same precepts governed the design of his pattern papers for the Curwen Press.[11]

Nash's achievement so far, though ambitious in its degree of abstraction, belonged to a tradition that went back to the seventeenth and eighteenth centuries. For Nash, small pattern abstraction was a way of avoiding what he saw as the over-styled designs of William Morris's successors and the art nouveau, which he disliked.[12] On the other hand, it helped him steer clear of Bloomsbury's floral decorations of the 1920s, with their Matisse-inspired cheerfulness. The hallmark of Nash's work was tightness of design, density and austerity, and his results generally reflected the handmade, carved effect of the wood-engraved origins of most of his end-paper and textile work. Though not an admirer of the flat pattern design of the early Arts and Crafts Movement itself, which he regarded as, in different instances, medievalising, mannered and decadent, he was nonetheless in some ways part of the movement's succession. He was

[9] Paul Nash, 'Woodcut Patterns', *The Woodcut: an annual*, 1, London, 1927, p.33. The article is reprinted in Nash's *Room and Book*, New York, 1932.

[10] Darcy Braddell, 'The Textile Designs of Paul Nash', *Architectural Review*, October 1928.

[11] Some of these were reproduced alongside work of other designers in a book for which Nash wrote an introduction. This introduction – 'A Specimen Book of Pattern Papers Designed for and in use at the Curwen Press' – was reprinted as a chapter in *Room and Book*.

[12] This and other of Nash's views on the history of architecture and design are taken from *Room and Book*, chapter 2.

[13] These firms included Footprints and Modern Textiles in the 1920s and Cresta Silks from 1930.

as perplexed as Morris had been at how standards of workmanship were to be maintained in the age of mass production and the machine. An artist before anything else, the handmade set the standard that machine production had to live up to. Nash remained loyal in his support of hand-block textile designers who came to the fore in the 1920s, especially the Phyllis Barron–Dorothy Larcher partnership, that started in 1923 and was joined, in 1925, by Enid Marx on her graduation from the Royal College at the time that Nash was teaching in the design school there. As a textile designer, Nash was associated with firms that used hand-block techniques and which, within the possibilities of viable commercial practice, allowed artists the head in the design process and some monitoring role during production.[13] Nash was a demanding artist to work with, with a mistrust of business people that may have been justified but sparked public expressions of dissatisfaction and even contempt that led to entrenched positions and did not always contribute to his objectives. At the root of his being, Nash was an arts and crafts man who looked back to pre-industrial materials and craft methods. After leaving his parental home, he never lived in a modern house and the Nash's furniture, whether old or new, tended to be of high-quality, un-adorned woods, such as oak. Individual objects were not in themselves obvious expressions of style, but collectively Nash's

Paul Nash, *The Rye Marshes*, 1932.
Poster: The Shell Art Collection.

EVERYWHERE YOU GO

THE RYE MARSHES   PAUL NASH

YOU CAN BE SURE OF SHELL

domestic environment represented a clear preference for tradition, understatement and lack of ornamentation.

The critic R H Wilenski, in a review of *Room and Book*,[14] argued that Nash failed to understand that mass production was in its nature a mirror of democracy, and reprimanded him for implying that industry should accept any terms the artist chose to impose. Nash and Wilenski both saw that the Romantic movement, in the context of the industrial revolution, had excluded the artist from his craftsman's role in the pre-industrial world, and had left the artist outside the design process. Though both thought this was a bad thing, Nash felt that the artist should be allowed back into the process without sacrificing his privileged independence, while Wilenski (who had been an artist himself before turning to criticism) wanted a new, more equal relationship of co-operation. The text of Wilenski's criticism was that the despair Nash felt at the blindness of manufacturers to the artist's contribution was really a form of protection of the artist's privileged role. Wilenski questioned Nash's reference to the inability of the public 'to feel beauty in objects' in a civilisation where 'taste remains the culture of the very few'. Nash fully supported experimental design, but did not always see it as available for mass production. Wilenski felt that this undervalued the public, whom it was the responsibility of artists working with industry to help provide for. He also believed that 'the desire to purchase objects designed by first-rate creative artists is not limited, as Mr Nash supposes, to a small minority with an extra ration of culture; it exists among people with an average equipment of taste, but it can only be gratified, in present conditions, by people with an extra ration of money'.

In 'Modern English Furnishing' (1930), reprinted as 'The Modern Aesthetic' in *Room and Book*, Nash looks for 'the almost indefinable spirit of the English tradition', which he finds in the 'architecture and ornament of the Adam period' and the Bloomsbury squares, which are as much a part of the character of Englishness for him as 'the white oak woods of Sussex or the beech aisles of the Chilterns'.[15] In a book which includes a diatribe against Victorian 'invasions by foreign fashions',[16] bringing with them, Nash believed, a meaningless eclecticism of style, he looked here to associate things that could be regarded as both English and natural: the neo-Classicism of Robert Adam, Bloomsbury houses and squares, and the English countryside are grouped together because Nash saw them as unaffected and natural. They are the real England: Adam and Bloomsbury can be looked at in the same way as an oak wood in Sussex or a beech avenue in the Chilterns because they are the quasi-permanent parts of an English heritage which are not contaminated by style.

Nash's linking the Regency with the modern was not uncommon at that time. He quoted in *Room and Book* from John C Rogers's article in the *Architectural Review*, 'The Real English Tradition': 'If we are destined to pick up a thread from the past, surely the Regency style stands invitingly as a truly modern development, nipped in the bud while we built up and perfected the mechanical age, to be now resumed in a Renaissance which many feel to be imminent.'[17] Within a few years, a different link with Modernism would emerge, in the writings of Raymond McGrath, F R S Yorke, Morton Shand and, pivotally, Nikolaus Pevsner.[18] The English tradition that lay behind and supported Modernism would be found not in the Regency, as the last movement uncontaminated by industrialism, but in the first flowering of the post-industrial reaction: in Morris, the Arts and Crafts, Mackintosh and the Cotswold furniture makers. Even in 1932, Nash was aware of Morris and his succession, but did not recognise them as 'pioneers'. The Modernism of the Bauhaus and Le Corbusier was still too excitingly unfamiliar in England for it to be possible for them to be associated with anything else. They still needed to be seen as a clean break.

Nash's unequivocal championing of the radical design represented a second side to him. In 1930 he entered a competition run by the *Architectural Review* for the design of the London rooms of a mythical Glasgow shipbuilder, Lord Benbow.[19] Benbow was specified as sympathetic to the modern but had difficulty with abstraction; as a Glaswegian he was familiar with the work of Mackintosh. The winner of the competition was Raymond McGrath, whom Nash singled out for praise in the same year in his article 'Modern English Furnishing'. McGrath specified Nash in his submission as the provider of textiles. Nash himself was placed second, and specified Denham MacLaren, whom Nash also praised in his article as designer of his furniture. Nash was evidently perceived as related to a circle of architect/designers whose work was among the most radical in England.

An example of Nash's involvement in experimental design that was actually made was the glass bathroom he designed in 1932 for the dancer, Tilly Losch, at 35 Wimpole Street. The surfaces of stippled and mirrored glass giving tinted effects of purplish-grey and pink, the pink rubber floor, black bathroom fittings and chromed-steel accessories have a sense of unity that represent a remarkable achievement for an artist unaccustomed to working in three dimensions. The mirrored ceiling and coloured floor were as much a part of the design structure as the walls and fitments. Bathroom design was on the avant-garde agenda. Bathrooms and kitchens were design areas spotlighted for research by the Design and Industries Association when Frank Pick took over the presidency at the beginning of 1932. Later in the year, the *Architectural Review* published a survey by the architect F R S Yorke called the 'Modern Bathroom'[20] in which the accent was on luxury as much as modernity, and nothing illustrated there was as daring as Nash's was to be. Although

[14] In *Architectural Review*, June 1932.

[15] *Room and Book*, p.6.

[16] *Ibid.*, p.5.

[17] *Architectural Review*, November 1931.

[18] See Raymond McGrath, *The English House*, London, 1934; F R S Yorke, *The Modern House*, London, 1934, a digest of which accompanied the first of six articles: 'Scenario for a Human Drama' by P Morton Shand, *Architectural Review*, July 1934–February 1935; N Pevsner, *Pioneers of Modern Design*, London, 1936. Compared with these authors, Nash's contribution was brief, and what is intended here is a survey of material covered, not a direct comparison of writers.

[19] See *Architectural Review*, May and November 1930.

[20] See *Architectural Review*, October 1932.

Paul Nash, *Event on the Downs*, 1934.
Oil on canvas. Government Art Collection.

his bathroom must have been disconcerting to use because mirrors are used decoratively as well as functionally, are fitted to the ceiling as well as the walls, and would have led to surprising and unpredictable reflections, Nash's bathroom was an artist's work, and his wife Margaret, in the memoir she published after his death, commented that Tilly Losch's husband, the poet, art patron and eccentric, Edward James, commissioned Nash because he could not find an architect who would do an interesting enough design.[21]

The direction of Nash's painting changed in the mid-1930s as he withdrew somewhat from the abstraction that had helped nurture his design work and joined the English Surrealist group. At the same time émigrés from Europe, from Gropius onwards, brought an increased sense of the social responsibility of architecture and design as it had evolved at – especially – the Bauhaus. Nash remained an artist and an individualist. He did not share Read's interest in typical forms and the moral superiority of the clean, white pared-down shapes of modern architecture and design. Nor, as an artist, were his interests governed in the way a professional designer's would be by the satisfaction of the consumer, whom Nash does not pay much heed to in his writings on design. When faced with a choice between the hand-made and the legacy of the Arts and Crafts, and the modern and mass-produced, Nash's instinct was to go with the former.

[21] Francis Carr, 'A Thirties Bathroom', *Crafts*, 79, March–April 1986.

Murphy, Mass Production and Modernism: Gordon Russell 1929–40

JEREMY MYERSON

In September 1929, the Cotswold-based furniture firm, The Russell Workshops, changed its name to Gordon Russell Ltd and the following month opened a London showroom. Within weeks, that enterprise – and the company with it – was threatened with disaster. The Wall Street Crash had destroyed the market for higher-priced furniture and the lucrative trade in antiques, handmade glass and textiles for the American market, trades upon which the company had been founded.

The economic hardship in the early 1930s led to the realisation that the only way out of the crisis was to concentrate on selling lower-priced furniture in greater numbers, and Gordon Russell's court-ship of machine production needed to become a lasting relation-ship if the company was to survive. The problem, of course, was how to achieve this without sacrificing the commitment to quality on which the company had built its reputation. There was also a question of where to find the customers. At this critical point in 1931, a telephone call to Gordon Russell from an engineer by the name of Frank Murphy influenced the whole course of British industrial design.

Murphy had just started making radio sets and was looking for a better alternative to the radio cabinets currently available from cabinet-makers. Gordon Russell had been recommended to him by the two men who had played such a vital role in the furniture firm's development in the 1920s: Percy Wells and John Gloag. In *Designer's Trade*, Gordon Russell describes how Murphy and his aptly-named partner, Ted Power, came down to his Broadway factory to seek help.

He (Murphy) felt that radio was too complicated: he wanted simpler, better built cabinets which were as good as the sets. 'Look at this,' he said to us,

The Gordon Russell Furniture offices in
Broadway, Worcestershire, with shop sign
by Geoffrey Jellicoe.

*producing a portable cabinet, 'it's just a box. No ideas. Ted and I have spent
many hours trying to find out how we can keep these ugly knobs out of sight
without making them inaccessible but we haven't got anywhere.'*

Sets had to be in the dealers' shops well before Christmas and Murphy's own enterprise hung in the balance, as did the future of Gordon Russell Ltd. In a sense the two companies clung together in the early 1930s, united by a common dependence on innovation for survival and success. Gordon Russell and Frank Murphy were both visionaries, leading young, vibrant and little-understood companies through uncharted waters, and they quickly struck up a strong understanding. Dick Russell's training at the Architectural Association, which he never completed, proved crucial. He now possessed a design methodology capable of leading the Broadway factory into a new era of mass production. As Kate Baynes, Gordon's daughter, comments: 'The difference was that while Gordon learnt in the workshop, Dick learnt at the drawing board. Dick has never received the true recognition he deserved for his work on Murphy radios.'

Although Gordon had virtually stopped designing, he had a large hand in the design of the very first radio cabinet for Murphy. This model was christened the 'Pentonville' by sceptical dealers, because one of its design features was a grill. Murphy's advertising slogan, 'Making Wireless Simple', was printed on all its packaging. Dick was responsible for all subsequent designs during the 1930s. These were increasingly characterised by clean lines and purist forms with no adornment or unnecessary detail. They are now widely recognised as classic designs of the period.

Within a couple of years, Dick Russell's designs for Murphy were beginning to influence other manufacturers. Reviewing the annual *Radiolympia* exhibitions in September 1933 in *Gramophone* magazine, writer P Wilson noted: 'Mr Russell has simply swept the board. I should hate to ascribe to him some of the monstrous developments that have been made from his clean lines and simple beauty of form. But even these exaggerations are in their way a tribute to his success.'

The more the radio cabinets distanced themselves from the decorative flavour of the first model, uncluttered by bars, frets or grills, the more they were responsible for introducing a new spare and modern visual language into British industrial design during the 1930s. Though not such a keen devotee as his brother Dick, Gordon Russell was interested in the Modern Movement's ideas on architecture and design, and during a visit to the celebrated Stockholm Exhibition of 1930, designed by Gunnar Asplund, he had been exposed to the latest in functional Modernism. It was in Stockholm that he also met the legendary Finnish designer, Alvar Aalto, whose furniture he later stocked in his London showroom.

However, as the architectural historian Nikolaus Pevsner has pointed out in *Studies in Art, Architecture and Design*, adoption of this new modern style, whether in furniture or radio cabinets, posed problems in production for Gordon Russell Ltd: 'The flush surfaces, the square legs, the exact unmitigated angles partook of the connotations of machine precision which played such a significant part in the modern style of architecture.'

Gordon Russell himself recognised that the hand skills of the old cabinet-makers at Broadway were not precise enough. As he explained in Designer's Trade: 'The [Murphy] engineers, accustomed to working in thousands of an inch, laughed at our idea of a tolerance: a sixteenth of an inch was a crevasse to them! They said we must learn to be accurate, wood or no wood.' The experience of producing cabinets for Murphy revolutionised the working methods of the company. Its tradition of craftsmanship and commitment to quality became wedded to high standards of engineering in wood. All measurements had to be taken from the inside instead of the outside. Along with greater mechanisation, the company introduced a scientific precision and consistency of manufacture which have been maintained ever since.

For a furniture company to take this route was highly unusual. In his 'Skill' lecture, Gordon Russell recalled how one of his peers reacted to the news:

My entry into this trade led Ambrose Heal, a good friend of mine and a member of the Arts and Crafts, to ring up with astonishment and disapproval in his voice to say: 'I hear you are making radio cabinets!' 'Yes', I said, 'a fascinating job. I expect that it may be all that we are remembered by!'

Also unusual was the role of Dick Russell in making an aesthetic input as an industrial designer on a par with and at the same time as electrical, mechanical and production engineers. Each radio set was designed in its entirety both inside and out before tooling began. Frank Murphy had broken the mould. Until the day he turned up at Broadway, the wireless industry norm had been to design a set and then buy a cabinet from a range of sketches submitted by a woodworking firm. Gordon Russell was not slow to grasp the significance of this. Murphy was a manufacturer using industrial design not as add-on decoration or ornament, but to shape the product's formal qualities. Russell wrote in *Designer's Trade*: 'Good industrial design goes down to the roots – it is never something added at the end.'

It was no surprise that Dick Russell became Murphy Radio's in-house designer, assisted by Eden Minns, another Architectural Association graduate. In 1935, Gordon Russell had opened a new factory at Park Royal in West London to cope with the growing radio production demands. The facade was designed by Geoffrey Jellicoe. At its peak in the late 1930s the factory employed 800 staff and made cabinets for Ekco, Bush, Ultra and Pye, as well for Murphy.

The importance of Murphy Radio to the development of Gordon Russell Ltd as a manufacturer in the 1930s cannot be overstated. While the retail trade made losses, radio production kept the company afloat: 40,000 sets of one model alone were manufactured. Company records for 1937 show that Gordon Russell made 200,000 radio cabinets in just one year. Not that the new-style designs were universally popular with the conservative trade and indifferent public. Even Murphy's own dealers and sales staff 'loathed Dick's designs,' according to a letter from C R Casson, Murphy's advertising agent. 'They may be fine design, modern, beautiful,' harassed Murphy reps used to argue, '. . . but even if they are beautiful they are out of place in the homes of people buying radio sets.' Frank Murphy was evidently unmoved by opposition to his design policy, while Gordon Russell remarked wryly of the episode in his 'Skill' lecture: 'We discovered that the public were greatly interested in the quality of the sets and would even accept a well-designed cabinet if the set was OK. This did not happen with wardrobes which had to be sold neat.'

On the furniture side, things were predictably as problematic as ever for a manufacturer pioneering modern design at a time when reproduction pieces were so popular. In any case, business was generally depressed in the early 1930s. But the Murphy radio work broadened the company's technological horizons. The contract introduced a new mood of flexibility and confidence into the factory, and had a profound effect on the type of work taken on subsequently. In fact it was crucial to survival, for the high engineering demands of radio production prepared the ground for the war work of the 1940s when Gordon Russell Ltd, unlike so many other manufacturers, managed to stay in business by making a wide range of military items – from ammunition boxes and Mosquito wing parts to high-precision aircraft models for wind-tunnel testing.

The 1930s marked a dynamic tension within Gordon Russell Ltd between two very different cultures in furniture-making. On one side was the cabinet-making tradition epitomized by Shoreditch-trained W H 'Curly' Russell, who became chief designer in 1934 and held the post for the next 35 years. On the other was the modern architectural approach being developed by Dick Russell and his friends from the Architectural Association. In the centre stood Gordon, who clearly embraced the new, while always acknowledging his debt to the old. Curly, too, took on board many of the new AA-inspired ideas in his work.

By the time Dick Russell had moved to London in 1932 – it was deemed convenient to have a director both resident in the capital and close to Murphy Radio's Welwyn Garden City headquarters – he

Room setting featuring 'Boomerang' rug
by Marian Pepler, Wellbeck sideboard, 1934,
by R D Russell, and chair by W H Russell.

had already stamped his mark on the company's design direction. The way in which Dick Russell's contribution was integrated into the product development process established an important precedent for British designers, who were increasingly being recognized as a profession in their own right, and had set up their own Society of Industrial Artists and Designers in 1930 (later renamed the Chartered Society of Designers). Gordon always admired his brother and encouraged him, so sharing to some extent a design education he never had. But Gordon also appreciated the value of Curly Russell, who, as his design assistant, had so skilfully interpreted his designs in the 1920s. The international reputation that Gordon Russell Ltd enjoyed in the 1930s was due, in no small part, to the subtle blend of cultures which brought so many different staff and consultant designers into the company.

The two cultures expressed themselves in the Broadway showrooms. L J Smith, a furniture salesman who joined the company in 1931, recalls how Dick Russell's modern designs were placed at the front of the showroom, while a back room was piled high with earlier Gordon Russell designs in the Gimson tradition that could not be sold. These expensive, ornate pieces with ebony and walnut inlays were considered out-of-date and were sometimes simply given to investors in the company such as William Cadbury or Cecil Pilkington. Yet today it is these very pieces that fetch high prices at auction.

Antiques were still sold at Broadway in the early 1930s, but the trade was so badly hit by the American Depression that Henry Keil, the company's antiques buyer, left Gordon Russell Ltd. Keil later set up his own business and became famous for antiques in Broadway. According to L J Smith, 'The only Americans who travelled around the Cotswolds in the early 1930s were teachers spending their life savings.' Things got so bad in 1933 that Gordon Russell decided to cut the salaries of all staff, including his own, by 10 per cent. L J Smith remembers that Gordon traded in his car for a small and cramped Austin, more in keeping with the austerity of the time. 'The sight of such a big man in that small car was ridiculous,' says L J Smith. 'The steering wheel came up to his knees.'

Despite the economic pressures there were light interludes. When business improved, Gordon rewarded the staff's loyalty and perseverance by sending a group of them, including L J Smith, Curly Russell, R H Bee and Ted Ould, on a cruise for three weeks to study architecture and furniture in northern capitals such as Danzig, Copenhagen and Stockholm. It was evidently a memorable trip, and a characteristically warm gesture on the part of the proprietor. L J Smith recalls that much effort was also put into staff activities. There were football matches between the Broadway and Park Royal factories, and large dinners afterwards. Even Gordon Russell himself, who could be a very shy and reserved man, engaged in such antics as imitating a coarse French porter during an office trip to France for the 1937 Paris International Exhibition, where the company was showing a room set designed by Curly Russell and Marian Pepler. It was at the end of the 1930s that the staff magazine, *The Circular Saw*, became a lively forum for debate.

The Russell family had now become the largest employer in Broadway. When L J Smith started work there in 1931, there were 200 staff in the factory and nearly 20 in the offices and showrooms. Smith remembers being summoned in fear and trembling to Gordon's office on his first day, but Gordon simply wanted to show him the Lygon Arms and buy him a pint of beer. Despite its expansion and mechanization, the enterprise remained very much a family firm. When a blaze in June 1934 gutted ten thatched cottages built for workers at the factory, it was a disaster not just for the company but for the entire area. After the fire was put out, S B Russell wrote to the local paper, describing the many offers of help for the ten homeless families as 'a magnificent triumph of practical sympathy and goodwill by the whole village'.

In the early days, Toni Russell, Gordon's wife, played a leading role in running the showrooms at Broadway, taking responsibility for buying in factored goods such as glass, fabrics, carpets and china to complement the furniture. In October 1933, Marian Pepler, who was based with Dick in London (they married in December), took over the job and became responsible for factored goods in both the Broadway and the 28 Wigmore Street showrooms. Marian had been encouraged by Dick to design rugs and carpets in a new geometric modern style that would complement his furniture and interior designs. Working for such manufacturers as Wilton Royal, Alexander Morton and Tomkinsons, her work swiftly came to public attention. It was commended for its grace and originality, and promoted by Gordon Russell Ltd in its advertising for complete room settings. Her first rug, in 1930, had been called Snowshill, in honour of the village in which Dick Russell's parents lived. When she and Dick Russell designed the Lobden house for Albert Hartley in 1932, four rugs – two circular and two rectangular – were specially designed for the interiors.

During the slump of 1933, the first Gordon Russell showroom, run by Ted Ould at 28 Wigmore Street, was set to close. As the company's financial chief, R H Bee, observed in a sales report, the shop was not attracting passing trade and was only taking orders from existing customers who had previously ordered direct from Broadway. But at that point Dick Russell, who had set up a design studio with Marian Pepler in the basement of the shop, intervened. He argued passionately that the showroom should remain open with key modifications to the retail strategy. In a report to the board, Dick Russell wrote: 'The shop falls between two stools by being neither a specialist decorator dealing exclusively in rather highly-priced and precious furniture and furnishings nor a furniture shop with a comprehensive stock at all prices.' His solu-tion was to produce and sell cheaper furniture ranges while at the same time improving the showroom display to attract a better class of customer. The shop was to feature entire room sets, and not simply a window display.

The company was now beginning to ride out the storm of the early 1930s. Sales of rugs, curtains and simple, modern, low-cost unit furniture ranges designed by Dick Russell were selling well enough to warrant more retail space, and Gordon Russell Ltd began to expand its retail business in the capital. The move to larger premises at 40 Wigmore Street, again rented from Debenhams, was therefore a logical conclusion of this upturn. Gordon Russell asked Geoffrey Jellicoe – who was closely associated with the company throughout the 1930s – to design the showroom, which had been used by Debenhams as a warehouse. Jellicoe installed a simple plate-glass frontage, lit the fascia lettering with pale-blue neon tubes, and punc-tuated the 120-foot length of the showroom with a series of indirectly-lit bays. Indeed, the entire lighting of the shop was most ingenious and provided a dramatic illuminated set piece for late-night audiences leaving the concerts at the nearby Wigmore Hall. Inside, the sense of modernity was tangible: there was no counter, and customers could sit on the furniture and touch the textiles. Marian Pepler's Aquamarine rug took pride of place in the window alongside Dick Russell's furniture.

The new shop was opened at the end of 1935 with a press and private view. Ted Ould had been promoted to the board of Gordon Russell Ltd and put in charge of contracts, so the job of running the London showroom was given to L J Smith. He recalls that his brief was clear: to sell more of the company's factory-made products and make the showroom seem less like a society interior decorator. Geoffrey Jellicoe's showroom design worked superbly to this end. The architect describes it as 'one of the most pleasing projects I've ever done. Gordon had a very clear mind which resulted in a very clear brief. We worked harmoniously together.'

Nikolaus Pevsner, who in *Studies in Art, Architecture and Design* describes Marian Pepler's rug designs as having 'a sensitivity and quiet perfection not surpassed anywhere in Europe', took her place as the company's chief buyer in 1936, shortly after the opening of 40 Wigmore Street. Pevsner had arrived in Britain two years earlier as a refugee from the rise of Nazism. He had been forced to give up his job in Dresden Art Gallery, but immediately came to Gordon Russell's attention when he undertook a year's research study at Birmingham University into the design of products for British industry. In compiling his survey, Pevsner visited hundreds of manufacturers. The factory at Broadway was one of them. In 1935, when Pevsner gave a lecture on his findings to the Design and Industries Association, Gordon Russell had been in the audience. According to *Designer's Trade*: 'He (Pevsner) showed such a comprehensive grasp of the subject that I went over to Birmingham the next day and asked him if he would like to buy textiles, rugs, glass and so on for us. Although he had never been in business, he said he would like to consider it.'

Pevsner worked for Gordon Russell until 1939, when he left to become the assistant editor of the *Architectural Review*, a post which set him on the road to become one of the finest art and architecture critics of the modern age. The fact that such an unusually gifted and well-informed writer should remain with the company for so long reflected Gordon Russell's ability to attract and retain the brightest young talents in British design. The company was undoubtedly an exciting place to be in the late 1930s, and Pevsner expressed an enormous respect and admiration for its achievements in his subsequent writing. Years later, when he was awarded the Gold Medal by the Royal Institute of British Architects in 1967, his celebration dinner was in Broadway as a guest of Gordon Russell.

Immediately after joining the team at 40 Wigmore Street, Pevsner added fine German wallpapers and fabrics to the ranges on sale. L J Smith thought it 'absurd that a fellow of Pevsner's knowledge and horizons should be restricted to fabrics', so Pevsner bought in Thonet bentwood chairs from Czechoslovakia as well as furniture by Alvar Aalto and Bruno Mathsson. Jewish refugees from Nazism living in nearby Hampstead were particularly good customers of the new showroom, as were stage folk such as Robert Donat and Charles Laughton. But as the war years drew near, Pevsner's cosmopolitan buying policy came in for criticism from the workforce at Broadway. Not only was the foreign furniture considered unpatriotic, but the construction of some of it ran counter to the best traditions of English cabinet-making. The issue was raised in the April 1939 edition of *The Circular Saw* by two cabinet shop workers, Adriaan Hermsen and P J Wade: 'Surely the sale of these articles aggravates our own employment problem,' they wrote. Pevsner was requested by editor Val Freeman to answer his critics immediately. He did so with masterful lucidity:

We don't bend solid beechwood as Thonet's have done for eighty years. Climatic conditions would not, I am told, favour such an industry. The design is good and clear, and the construction sound. We don't bend ply either, at least not in our cabinet shops. Aalto, the Finnish architect, has made a name all over Europe for this particular technique and these logically designed and made shapes . . . As long as such limitations of manufacturing and of style exist in our production – and are they not bound to exist always and everywhere? – I am afraid 95% British is as far as we can go: in furniture that is to say. Fabrics would be quite a different story.

The London showroom remained open until 1940, when, in the words of L J Smith, 'there was nothing left to sell'. The Broadway factory had been turned over to war work and Smith himself was directed to chase payment for defence contracts from government departments. He remembers an unsuccessful visit to the Navy accounts department at Blackheath to see if a Gordon Russell Ltd invoice could be paid. It was a far cry from an earlier engagement with the Navy in 1938, when L J Smith supervised a Gordon Russell contract to furnish the quarters of the King and Queen on board HMS *Repulse*.

Despite its inevitable closure by the time of the Blitz, Gordon Russell's London showroom at 40 Wigmore Street played its full part in the brief flowering of Modernism in Britain in the late 1930s. It was an exciting time for Dick Russell and Marian Pepler, who were then living at the famous Highpoint flats in Highgate, designed by Berthold Lubetkin. As standard-bearers for modern design, they were very much at the centre of the movement. Their friends included Hugh Casson, Ambrose Heal, Oliver Hill, Misha Black, Wells Coates and F R S Yorke. Gordon Russell's own position was more ambivalent. He was undeniably one of the most active and conspicuous patrons of modern design in Britain, yet, as Marian Pepler explains: 'He stood back from the Modern Movement, aloof from it. He didn't want to embrace it. Essentially he remained a supporter of the Art Workers' Guild.'

Nevertheless overseas visitors to the factory at Broadway in the 1930s included the Japanese ceramicist Shoji Hamada, Bernard Leach, Harold Stabler, American industrial designers Walter Dorwin Teague and Gilbert Rhode, and Bauhaus émigrés Walter Gropius and Marcel Breuer. Gordon had joined the community of the world's leading design names and was clearly able to discuss his company's aspirations on equal terms.

In 1939 storm clouds were gathering in more ways than one. Many of Gordon Russell's initiatives, including the formation in 1938 of the Good Furnishing Group, comprising a body of like-minded retailers, were soon cut short by war. Design had been given its head within the company during the 1930s but, as trading conditions deteriorated rapidly, the company's financial affairs began to unravel. Minutes of board meetings in the late 1930s are littered with

R D Russell,
Murphy radio cabinets and television cabinets manufactured by Gordon Russell Ltd, 1930s.

talk of 'crisis' and 'desperate measures'. Gordon's strong streak of idealism meant that he was not able to balance compromises in technical quality and visual standards against the need to survive financially. In the July 1940 edition of *The Circular Saw*, he wrote under the heading 'Great Britain versus Boche and Wops':

The Directors wish to make clear that they are reducing the two retail shops and turning over to still more war work as rapidly as possible. Don't be impatient. Even with the present spurt there is not a vast amount of war woodwork, and some of the other work we are doing such as radio is of national importance.

But three months later he was forced to resign as managing director of the company. The bank was threatening to withdraw support if R H Bee was not appointed in his place to run Gordon Russell Ltd. Gordon retired to his garden at Kingcombe in October 1940 and never again held an executive position in the company. He had been managing director for just seven years (having taken over from his father in 1933), but in that short time he had established an international reputation for the Broadway factory. According to Trevor Chinn, who joined the company in 1938 as an apprentice and was chief designer at Gordon Russell Ltd from 1969 to 1988, the success of the company in the 1930s was 'due to the strong mix of in-house and external designers working together. An ethos developed which continues today.'

Autumn 1940 not only marked the withdrawal of Gordon Russell from the company. On the night of the German raid on Coventry, a stray incendiary bomb from a German war plane landed on the great barn at Broadway. The thatched roof immediately caught fire. Inside, stockpiles of fine furniture and textiles brought from London for safe storage were destroyed. Amongst the furniture was, ironically, a large order for Sir John Anderson, Minister for Air Raid Precautions. Gordon later wrote, 'Our world was indeed disintegrating.'

Note

This essay was published first in Jeremy Myerson's *Gordon Russell: designer of furniture 1892–1992*, Design Council, London, 1992, ISBN 0852 072 306X, and appears by kind permission of the author, Gordon Russell Ltd and Gower Publishing.

Who was Who 1929–39: a Selected List

Armstrong, John (1893-1973)

Painter, designer. First one-man show at Leicester Gallery, 1931. Designs for ballet *Facade*, 1931. Member of Unit One, 1933. Designed costumes for Korda films including *The Private Life of Henry VIII*, 1935, *I Claudius*, 1937. Tableware designs for A J Wilkinson, Royal Staffordshire Pottery, 1934.

Arup, Ove (1895-1988)

Structural engineer. Born in Newcastle to Danish parents, returned to England as an engineer specialising in concrete. Acted as consulting engineer to Lubetkin for design of Gorilla House, Penguin Pool, Highpoint and other buildings. Established international interdisciplinary engineering practice, Ove Arup & Partners after the war.

Auden, W H (1907-1973)

Poet and writer. Friend and collaborator of Stephen Spender. Published first volume of poems in 1930. Librettist of Benjamin Britten operas including *Paul Bunyan*. Made documentary film for the GPO entitled *Night Mail*. With Christopher Isherwood wrote book on China in 1939, *Journey to a War*, and a number of plays. Professor of poetry at Oxford University, 1956–61.

Banting, John (1902-1972)

Painter. Designed book jackets for Hogarth Press and Sadler's Wells ballet. Exhibited at International Surrealist Exhibition, 1936. Art Director for Strand Films, 1939.

Barman, Christian (1898-1980)

Architect, designer, writer. Studied architecture at Liverpool. Editor of *Architects' Journal* and *Architectural Review*. Publicity Officer, London Passenger Transport Board, 1935–41. Wrote biography of Frank Pick, *The Man who Built London Transport*, 1979.

Barron and Larcher

Textile designers and printers, Phyllis Barron (1890-1964) and Dorothy Larcher (1884-1952). Printed textiles for dresses and soft furnishing in Hampstead studios until 1930, then Painswick, Gloucestershire.

Bernal, J D (1901-1971)

Scientist, polymath. His work in crystallography established the shape of viruses and proteins. Author of *The Social Function of Science*, 1939. Friend of Barbara Hepworth.

Best, Robert Dudley (1892-1984)

Designer and manufacturer of light fittings and architectural metalwork. Studied in Düsseldorf and Paris. Influenced by Walter Gropius. Managing Director of Best & Lloyd Ltd, Smethwick.

Betjeman, John (1906-1984)

Poet, architectural and topographical writer. Assistant editor of *Architectural Review*, 1930–5. Founder editor of *Shell Country Guides*, 1934. Member of MARS Group. Interested by early 1930s in rediscovering survivors of the Arts and Crafts Movement. Later Poet Laureate.

Black, Misha (1910-1977)

Designer. Born in Russia, he was brought by his parents to Britain aged 18 months. Exhibition designer from 1928. Established Studio Z in 1930. In 1933 he joined the Bassett-Gray Group of Artists and Writers which became the Industrial Design Partnership, 1935–40, Britain's first multidisciplinary design studio.

Brandt, Bill (1904-1983)

Photographer. Documented many aspects of British life in the 1930s. Work includes *The English at Home*, 1936.

Breuer, Marcel (1902-1981)

Architect, furniture designer, educationalist. Hungarian-born. Director of furniture workshop at the Bauhaus, 1925–8. Moved to England, 1934. In practice with F R S Yorke, 1935–7. Designed furniture for Isokon. Moved to USA, 1937.

Burra, Edward (1905-1976)

Painter. member of Unit One, 1933. Work included in International Surrealist Exhibition, London, 1936 and *Fantastic Art, Dada and Surrealism* at the Museum of Modern Art, New York, 1936. Also designed ballet sets.

Chermayeff, Serge (1900-1996)

Architect, furniture and interior designer. Russian-born. Moved to England, 1910. Director of Waring & Gillow's Modern Art Studio 1928-3. Independent practice 1931-3. Member of MARS Group in partnership with Eric Mendelsohn, 1933–6 with whom he designed the De la Warr Pavilion, Bexhill-on-Sea. Independent practice, 1937–9. Moved to USA, 1939.

Clarke Hall, Denis (b.1911)

Architect. Specialised in educational buildings.

Coates, Wells (1895-1958)

Architect, interior and industrial designer. Born in Japan to Canadian parents. Studied engineering in Vancouver and London. Work includes flats at Lawn Road and Princes Gate, London, BBC Studios in London and Newcastle, Ekco radio. Member of Twentieth Century Group, Unit One; founder member of MARS Group.

Coldstream, William (1908-1987)

Painter. Member of London Artists' Association, 1933. Worked for GPO Film Unit 1934–7. Involved with Euston Road School, 1937. Worked for Mass Observation Unit in Bolton, 1938.

Connell, Ward and Lucas

Architects. Amyas Connell (1901-1980), Basil Ward (1902-1976) and Colin Lucas (1906-1984). Work included houses at Amersham, Hampstead, Ruislip, etc. Connell and Ward partnership formed in 1931, Lucas joined in 1933. Partnership dissolved 1939.

Cooper, Susie (1902-1995)

Ceramic designer. Best known for decorated earthernwares. Started her own firm, 1929. Exhibited in British section of Paris International Exhibition, 1937. Imperial Airways commissioned tableware, 1937–8.

Crabtree, William (1905-1991)

Architect. Research architect for John Lewis Partnership, 1930. Worked on scheme for Peter Jones store, 1933–5. Worked on John Lewis store, Cavendish Square, 1936–9.

Dobson, Frank (1888-1963)

Sculptor, textile designer. Ceramic reliefs for Hay's Wharf, 1930. Designed screen-printed soft furnishings for Allan Walton textiles as well as his own block-printed fabrics.

Dorn, Marion (1899-1964)

Textile designer. Designed carpets and textiles for The Savoy, Claridges, the Orion, Queen Mary, etc. Supplied designs to Warner & Sons Ltd, Old Bleach Linen Company and Edinburgh Weavers. Established Marion Dorn Ltd in 1934.

Ede, H S 'Jim' (1895-1990)

Assistant curator, Tate Gallery, 1922–36. Friend and supporter of contemporary English artists. Author of *Savage Messiah* (life of Henri Gaudier-Brzeska), 1931. Lived in Tangier 1936–40. After the war, created Kettles Yard, Cambridge, a house with works of art which was donated to the University.

Elmhirst, Leonard (1893-1974) and Dorothy (1887-1968)

Educationalists. Married in 1911. Established a pioneering liberal school at Dartington Hall, where teachers included Bernard Leach and Mark Tobey. Friends and patrons of many leading modernist architects and artists. Commissioned a design proposal for an Open Air Theatre at Dartington Hall by Walter Gropius, 1935.

Emberton, Joseph (1889-1956)

Architect. Work includes Royal Corinthian Yacht Club (Burnham-on-Crouch), 1930–2; Simpson's Piccadilly, 1933–4; Blackpool Pleasure Beach buildings, 1933; and HMV building, Oxford Street, 1938–9.

Evans, Merlyn Oliver (1910-1973)

Painter, sculptor, engraver. Studied at Royal College of Art, 1931–3. In Paris 1934–6. Represented in Abstract and Non-Figurative Art Exhibition, Paris, 1936, and International Surrealist Exhibition, London, 1936. *Nine Abstract Art Books* exhibition, 1939.

Farleigh, John (1900-1965)

Wood engineer, painter. Best known for book illustrations such as Butler's *The Way of All Flesh,* 1934; D H Lawrence's *The Man Who Died,* 1935.

Fry, E Maxwell (1899-1987)

Architect. Founder member of MARS Group. In partnership with Walter Gropius, 1934–6. Practised with his wife, Jane Drew, 1945–50 and as Fry, Drew, Drake and Lasdun, 1950–8. Work includes Kensal House, London; Village College, Impington (with Gropius).

Gabo, Naum (1890-1977)

Sculptor. Born in Russia, lived in Berlin, 1922–32. Pioneer of constructivist sculpture. Experimented with new materials like perspex. Met Ben Nicholson and Barbara Hepworth in Paris and moved to St Ives in Cornwall in 1932. Important influence on a generation of St Ives artists. Broadcaster for the BBC during the war years.

Gibberd, Frederick (1908-1984)

Architect. Member of MARS Group. Worked on Analysis of Bethnal Green and 1938 exhibition. Work includes Park Court (Crystal Palace), 1936, Nurses' Home, Macclesfield, 1937–9.

Gill, Eric (1882-1940)

Sculptor, engraver, typographer. Sculptures for Broadcasting House, 1929–31; League of Nations Building, Geneva, 1936.

John Gloag (1896-1981)

Writer. Author of more than 80 books, many on design and architecture. Active in the Design and Industries Association. Populariser in England of American ideas on design and champion of new materials like plastics.

Goldfinger, Ernö (1902-1987)

Architect, furniture and interior designer. Born in Budapest. Moved to London, 1934. Member of MARS Group. Work includes house at Broxted, 1937, houses at Willow Road, London, 1937–9.

Gollancz, Victor (1893-1967)

Publisher. Founded own imprint in 1928 and employed Stanley Morison to design yellow typographic jackets. Founded Left Book Club in 1936, for social policy at home and resistance to Nazism and Fascism abroad.

Goodhart-Rendell, H S (1887-1959)

Architect. Director of Architectural Association School, 1936–8. President of RIBA, 1937–9. Work includes Hay's Wharf, London 1929–31; St Wilfred, Brighton, 1933–4; St Mary, East Hounslow 1937–40.

Grigson, Geoffrey (1905-1985)

Writer. Editor of *New Verse,* 1934–9, the most critical literary magazine of the 1930s. Editor of the symposium *The Arts Today,* 1935. Contributed to *Axis* and involved in the rediscovery of English romantic art.

Gropius, Walter (1883-1969)

Architect, furniture designer. Born in Germany, moved to England, 1934. Founded the Bauhaus at Weimar in 1919. Worked in association with Maxwell Fry, 1934–6, then in partnership, 1936–7. Moved to USA, 1937. In partnership with Marcel Breuer, 1938–41. Work includes processing labora-tories, Denham; Village College, Impington; furniture designs for Isokon.

Havinden, Ashley (1903-1973)

Graphic and textile designer, painter. Director of Art and Design at W S Crawford advertising agency, 1929. Commissions included work for Milk Marketing Board, GPO, Simpson's Piccadilly. Rug and textile designs for J Duncan Miller, 1933, Edinburgh Weavers, Campbell Fabrics and Wilton, 1937.

Hepworth, Barbara (1903-1975)

Sculptor. Worked with Ben Nicholson, 1931 onwards (and subsequently married). Exhibited at Lefevre Gallery, 1932, 1933. Member of the Seven and Five Society, 1931–5. Member of Abstraction-Creation, 1933. Member of Unit One, 1933–5. Collaborated with Nicholson and Edinburgh Weavers on range of 'constructionist fabrics'.

Hill, Oliver (1887-1968)

Architect. Work includes Midland Hotel, Morecambe, 1931–2, industrial art exhibition at Dorland Hall, 1933, scheme for Frinton Park Estate and seafront development, 1934–5, British Pavilion at Paris International Exhibition, 1937.

Hitchens, Ivon (1893-1979)

Painter. Member of the Seven and Five Society, 1921–35 and the London Group, 1931. *Objective Abstractions* at Zwemmer Gallery, 1934.

Holden, Charles (1875-1960)

Architect. Commissioned by Frank Pick to design new fronts for existing underground stations such as St Paul's and Mansion House, and new stations on Morden extension of Northern Line. Sudbury Town station, 1931, established new house style. Involved in development scheme for London University, 1931 onwards.

Isherwood, Christopher (1904-1986)

Novelist, playwright. Left-wing writer whose travels in Germany during the Weimar Republic influenced many of his books including *Goodbye to Berlin*, 1939. Worked on Hollywood filmscripts from 1933. With W H Auden wrote a book on China in 1939, *Journey to a War*, and a number of plays. Settled in California in 1939.

Jellicoe, Geoffrey (1900-1996)

Landscape architect. Wrote extensively on garden design. Designed showrooms for Gordon Russell Ltd and the Caveman restaurant at Cheddar Gorge with architect Russell Page, 1934.

Jennings, Humphrey (1907-1950)

Film maker, painter, poet. Joined GPO Film Unit, 1934. *The Spirit of the Robot*, 1936. Included in International Surrealist Exhibition, London, 1936. Founder of Mass Observation 1937–8. Rejoined GPO Film Unit, 1938. *Spare Time* and *The First Days*, 1939.

Kauffer, Edward McKnight (1890-1954)

Graphic designer. US-born, moved to England, 1914. Produced poster designs for London Transport Board, Shell-Mex, Great Western Railway, Orient Line, etc. Also designed book jackets and rugs. Married to Marion Dorn.

Lasdun, Denys (b.1914)

Architect. Student at Architectural Association, 1931–4. Worked in association with Wells Coates, 1935–7; worked with Tecton, 1937–9. Work includes house in Newton Road, London, 1937–8.

Leach, Bernard (1887-1979)

Potter. Discovered pottery during residence in Japan. Returned to England 1920 and established his own studio. Began teaching at Dartington Hall (Devon), 1932.

Lescaze, William (1896-1969)

Architect. Swiss-born. Work includes buildings for Dartington Hall Estate (Devon), 1931–6.

Livett, R A H (1898-1959)

Architect. With Nottingham Corporation, 1925–31. Deputy Director of Housing, Manchester, responsible for Wythenshawe Estate and for Smedley Point flats, Cheetham, 1931–4. Appointed Director of Housing, Leeds, responsible for Quarry Hill redevelopment, 1934.

Lubetkin, Berthold (1901-1990)

Architect. Georgian-born. Moved to England 1930. Formed Tecton in 1932. Member of MARS Group. For work, see Tecton.

Lucas, Colin

- see Connell, Ward and Lucas.

MacLaren, Denham (1903-1989)

Painter, furniture designer. After designing for Arundell Display, opened his own studio showroom in Davies Street in 1930. His glass and zebra skin chair and circular glass-topped table of 1931 are the most 'advanced' British furniture of the period. Moved into property management in late 1930s.

MacNeice, Louis (1907-1963)

Poet, teacher and broadcaster. Moved to the left during the 1930s. Wrote *Letters from Iceland* with W H Auden, 1937. Other works include *The Earth Compels*, 1938, and *Autumn Journal*, 1939.

Martin, Leslie (b.1908)

Architect. Student at School of Architecture, Manchester University, 1925–30, then lecturer there 1930–4. Head of School of Architecture, Hull College of Arts and Crafts, 1934–9. Work includes houses at Brampton, Ferriby, Rock, primary school at Northwich, designs for unit furniture.

Marx, Enid (1902-1998)

Textile designer, printmaker. Created hand block-printed textiles in her own studio until 1939. Commissioned by Frank Pick to design moquettes for London Transport, 1937.

McGrath, Raymond (1903-1977)

Architect, interior and industrial designer. Work includes BBC studios and offices, London and Manchester, 1930–2; radio cabinet designs for Ekco; aircraft interiors for Imperial Airways; Fischers' Restaurant, 1932; Embassy Club, 1933; houses at Chertsey, 1935–7; houses at Gaulby, 1936–9.

McWilliam, F E (1909-1992)

Sculptor. At Slade 1928–31. Paris, 1931–2. First sculpture, 1933. British Surrealist Group, 1938. *Living Art in England*, London Gallery; first one-man show, London Gallery, 1939.

Mendelsohn, Eric (1887-1953)

Architect. German-born. Moved to England, 1933. In practice with Chermayeff, 1933–6. Emigrated to USA, 1939. Work includes (with Chermayeff) De la Warr Pavilion, Bexhill-on-Sea, 1933–6; Nimmo house, Chalfont-St-Giles, 1934–5; Levy house, London, 1935–6.

Moholy-Nagy, László (1895-1946)

Painter, photographer, graphic designer and educationalist. Hungarian-born. Taught at Bauhaus, 1923–8. Worked in London, 1935–7. Emigrated to USA, 1937. Work includes posters for London Transport, Imperial Airways; publicity for Simpson's store and Isokon.

Moore, Henry (1898-1986)

Sculptor. Instructor in Sculpture Department, Royal College of Art, 1924–32. Commission for relief on St James's Park underground station building, 1928–9. Member of London Group, 1930–7. Member of Seven and Five Society, 1930–5. Member of Unit One, 1933. International Surrealist Exhibition, 1936. *Living Art in England*, London Gallery, 1939.

Morison, Stanley (1889-1967)

Typographer, typographic historian. Joined the staff of the printing journal *The Imprint* in 1913. Moved to the Pelican Press in 1919, where he wrote his first book on typography, *The Craft of Printing*, in 1921. Editor of *The Fleuron*, 1926–30. Typographic adviser to the Monotype Corporation, 1922–67 and Cambridge University Press, 1925–44. His support enabled Eric Gill's typefaces Perpetua, 1925, and Gill Sans to be produced. His classic text is *First Principles of Typography*, 1929.

Morton, Alistair (1910-1963)

Textile manufacturer, painter. Joined family firm, Morton Sundour Fabrics Ltd, 1931. Supervised first Sundour screen print range. Artistic Director of Edinburgh Weavers 1932 onwards.

Murray, Keith (1892-1981)

Glass, ceramic and silver designer, architect. Exhibited design work at Dorland Hall, 1933; Milan, 1933; Royal Academy, 1935; Victoria and Albert Museum, 1935. Started architectural practice in 1936, designed for Wedgwood and designed Wedgwood factory at Barlaston.

Murray, William Staite (1881-1961)

Ceramic designer. Head of Pottery School, Royal College of Art 1926 onwards. Moved to Southern Rhodesia in 1939.

Nash, Paul (1889-1946)

Painter, designer. War artist in both world wars. Founded Unit One, 1933. Designed tableware decoration for E Brain & Co, 1933–4. *Shell Guide to Dorset*, 1935. Contributed to *Axis*. Included in International Surrealist Exhibition, London, 1936, and New York World Fair, 1939.

Nicholson, Ben (1894-1982)

Painter, designer. Member of Seven and Five Society, 1924–36. Exhibited at Lefevre Gallery, 1932–9. Member of Unit One, 1933. Married to Barbara Hepworth.

Nicholson, Christopher (1904-1948)

Architect. Work includes studio for Augustus John, 1933–4; London Gliding Club, Dunstable, 1934–5; scheme for reconstruction of the Pantheon, 1938–9.

Orwell, George (1903-1950)

Novelist, journalist and political writer. After studying at Eton, joined the Burmese police. Major works of the 1930s include *Down and Out in Paris and London*, 1933; *Burmese Days*, 1934; *The Road to Wigan Pier*, 1937, and *Homage to Catalonia*, 1938.

Pepler, Marian (1904-1997)

Architect, rug and textile designer. Studied at the Architectural Association, 1924–9. Later trained at the London School of Weaving. Designed rugs and textiles for Gordon Russell Ltd, Royal Wilton and Alex Morton. Included in the International Exhibition in Paris, 1937. Married to R D Russell.

Pevsner, Nikolaus (1902-1983)

Historian of art, architecture and design. Born in Leipzig, gained a PhD in German Baroque architecture in 1924. Worked at the Dresden Gallery, 1924–9, lectured on British art at Göttingen University, 1929–33. Settled in Britain in 1933. Important champion of modernist architecture and design. Books include *Pioneers of the Modern Movement*, 1936, and *An Enquiry into Industrial Art in England*, 1937.

Pick, Frank (1878-1941)

Design patron. After studying law, Pick became publicity manager at London Passenger Transport Board in 1908 and eventually became chief executive of the entire organisation. He was a tireless champion of good modern design. He was responsible for raising the standard of every aspect of LPTB's design through commissioning architects like Charles Holden, artists and sculptors like Paul Nash and Eric Gill, and poster designers like Edward McKnight Kauffer. Appointed first chairman of the Council for Art and Industry. Founder and president of the Design and Industries Association.

Piper, John (1903-1992)

Painter, illustrator, designer. Member of London Group, 1933. Member of Seven and Five Society, 1934–5. Helped Myfanwy Evans (his second wife) to produce *Axis*, 1935-7. Wrote for *Architectural Press* and designed and provided photography for Shell Guides.

Pritchard, Jack (1899-1992)

Furniture manufacturer. Founder of Isokon, a company which commissioned and built furniture designs by the leading modernist designers of the 1930s, including Marcel Breuer, Wells Coates and Gerald Summers. Commissioned the Lawn Road Flats by Wells Coates which became a magnet for émigré architects and artists like Breuer, Gropius and Moholy-Nagy.

Ravilious, Eric (1903-1942)

Wood-engraver, watercolourist. Taught by Paul Nash. Instructor at Royal College of Art, 1929–38. Numerous book illustrations, First commission from Wedgwood, 1935. Designed range of glass for Stuart Crystal, 1935. Designed wall decoration for British Pavilion at Paris Exhibition, 1937.

Read, Herbert (1893-1968)

Poet, anarchist and writer on art. Involved in the key artistic movements of the 1930s in England. Pulled between rationalism and romanticism. Books include *Art Now*, 1933; *Art and Industry*, 1934, and *Art and Society*, 1937. After the war, founded the Institute of Contemporary Art with Roland Penrose.

Richards, Ceri (1903-1971)

Painter, printmaker and stained-glass designer. Began to make pictorial relief constructions in 1934, some of which were in *Surrealist Objects*, London Gallery, 1937.

Russell, Gordon (1892-1980)

Furniture maker, designer. Began to design furniture c. 1910. Created Gordon Russell Ltd, 1926. Produced radio cabinets designed by his brother R D Russell for Frank Murphy, 1931, shown at Royal Academy, 1935, Paris exhibition, 1937. Launched the Good Furniture Group in 1938, a scheme to mass-produce furniture.

Skeaping, John (1901-1984)

Sculptor. Played important role in development of directly carved sculpture. Designed animal figures for Wedgwood in late 1920s. Member of Seven and Five Society. Married to Barbara Hepworth, 1925–33.

Spender, Humphrey (b.1910)

Photographer. Began 'Lensman' series for *Daily Mirror*, 1934. Photographer with Mass Observation in Bolton, 1937. With *Picture Post*, for which he created photo-surveys of cities from 1938 onwards.

Spender, Stephen (1909-1995)

Poet and writer. Studied at Oxford and then lived in Germany for two years. His *Poems*, 1933, allied him with W H Auden and Cecil Day Lewis. Wrote *Forward from Liberalism*, 1936, an early Left Book Club selection.

Stokes, Adrian (1902-1972)

Writer, painter. Wrote passionately about Italian architecture and sculpture in *The Quattro Cento*, 1932, and *Stones of Rimini*, 1934. Began painting in 1935 and attended Euston Road School. His book *Colour and Form*, 1937, based on analysis with Melanie Klein.

Summers, Gerald (1899-1967)

Designer. Designed bent plywood furniture for The Makers of Simple Furniture, of which he was a director. Some of his designs were made by Isokon. Later abandoned furniture and moved into the ball bearings industry.

Sutherland, Graham (1903-1980)

Painter, designer. Taught engraving at Chelsea College of Art, 1926–35. Tableware decoration for E Brain, Fennemore and A J Wilkinson 1933–4. Began painting in 1934. Included in International Surrealist Exhibition, London, 1936. First one-man show at Rosenberg and Helft, 1938. Designed glassware for Stuart and Sons.

Tait, Thomas (1882-1954)

Architect. Work includes Unilever House; Curzon Cinema; Empire Exhibition, Glasgow; Sydney Harbour bridge (as consultant).

Tecton

Architectural partnership formed 1932 by Lubetkin and Anthony Chitty (1907-1976), Lindsey Drake (1909-1980), Michael Dugdale (1906-1973), Valentine Harding (1905-1940), Godfrey Samuel (1904-1983) and R T F Skinner (1908-1973). Chitty, Dugdale, Harding and Samuel all left in 1935. Work includes buildings for Regent's Park, Whipsnade and Dudley zoos; Highpoint I and II (Highgate); Finsbury Health Centre.

Wadsworth, Edward (1889-1949)

Painter. Member of Unit One, 1933. Two paintings for Smoking Rooms on the Queen Mary, 1936. Designed mural for De la Warr Pavilion, Bexhill-on-Sea.

Ward, Basil

- see Connell, Ward and Lucas.

Williams, Owen (1890-1969)

Engineer. Work includes Boots factory, Beeston, 1930–2; *Daily Express* buildings at London, Manchester and Glasgow; Empire Pool, Wembley, 1933–4; Pioneer Health Centre, London, 1934–5; Dollis Hill synagogue, London, 1937–8.

Williams-Ellis, Clough (1883-1978)

Architect. Work includes extensions and alterations to Portmeirion; Laughing Water roadhouse, Cobham; Hirtwood School, Peaslake; First Church of Christ Scientist, Belfast; houses at Brickenden, Llanbedrog; Rhos-on-Sea.

Wolpe, Berthold (1905-1989)

Typographer, teacher. Born in Germany. Taught at the Frankfurt Kunstschule, 1929–33. At Stanley Morison's suggestion he designed the Albertus type for the Monotype Corporation in 1934, which was widely used for signage, books etc. Settled in England in 1935 and worked for Fanfare Press, designing book jackets for Victor Gollancz.

Yorke, F R S (1906-1962)

Architect. In practice with Marcel Breuer, 1935–7. Founder member of the MARS Group. Editor of *Specification*, 1935–62. Work includes houses at Gidea Park, Stratford-on-Avon, Bristol, Eton, Lee-on-Solent.

1929–1939: A Brief Chronology

ALAN POWERS

1929

Politics

MAY

General Election. Ramsay MacDonald forms second Labour government without overall majority. Government liberalises entitlement to benefits.

OCTOBER

Wall Street Crash. Diplomatic relations with Soviet Union restored.

DECEMBER

Empire Crusade launched by Lord Beaverbrook.

Architecture

Cresta Silks shops (Wells Coates)

Design

Modern Art in French and English Furniture and Decoration exhibition at Waring & Gillows, organised by Serge Chermayeff and Paul Follot (opened November 1928).

Exhibition of rugs by Marion Dorn and McKnight Kauffer, Tooth & Sons.

Susie Cooper establishes pottery in Burslem.

Literature/Music/Film

The Good Companions (J B Priestley)

Goodbye to all that (Robert Graves)

Death of a Hero (Richard Aldington)

Journey's End (Robert Sherriff)

Viola Concerto (William Walton)

Drifters (John Grierson)

1930

Politics

Housing ('Greenwood') Act and Housing (Scotland) Act: makes central government subsidies available for rehousing people affected by slum clearance schemes.

MAY

Resignation of Sir Oswald Mosley from government.

Art

MAY

Ben Nicholson and Christopher Wood exhibit in Paris.

AUGUST

Death of Christopher Wood.

Architecture

Foundation of Twentieth Century Group.

Cambridge Theatre (interiors by Serge Chermayeff)

New Empire Hall, Olympia (Joseph Emberton)

High & Over (Amyas Connell)

Crawfords Advertising, 233 High Holborn (Frederick Etchells)

Strand Palace Hotel Foyer (Oliver Bernard)

Stockholm Exhibition

Design

The Face of the Land (DIA).

Bestlite by Best & Lloyd of Smethwick.

Literature/Music/Film

Seven Types of Ambiguity (William Empson)

Ash Wednesday (T S Eliot)

Vile Bodies (Evelyn Waugh)

Private Lives (Noel Coward) .

The Apes of God (Wyndham Lewis)

Job, a masque for dancing (Ralph Vaughan-Williams)

Hammersmith (Gustav Holst)

Morning Heroes (Arthur Bliss)

Foundation of BBC Symphony Orchestra.

1931

Politics

FEBRUARY

Public-spending cuts proposed by Committe on National Expenditure.

MARCH

Formation of New party by Mosley.

JULY

European financial crisis, massive cuts in expenditure and pressure on sterling.

AUGUST

Collapse of Labour government. MacDonald forms National Government with support from Conservatives and other parties.

SEPTEMBER

Increase in taxes and reduction in public expenditure. Britain forced off gold standard.

OCTOBER

Split in Liberal Party.

NOVEMBER

Formation of Second National Government by MacDonald.

Trevelyan's Education Bill (raising school leaving age to 15) defeated in House of Lords.

Art

Genesis (Jacob Epstein)

SEPTEMBER

Meeting of Ben Nicholson and Barbara Hepworth at Happisburgh, Norfolk.

Room and Book exhibition at Zwemmer Gallery (organised by Paul Nash).

Architecture

Sudbury Town Station (Charles Holden)

Daily Express building, Fleet Street (Owen Williams)

Berthold Lubetkin settles in England.

Design

Makers of Simple Furniture (Gerald Summers)

Isokon Company established.

Literature/Music/Film

The Waves (Virginia Woolf)

Men and Wives (Ivy Compton Burnett)

Belshazzar's Feast (Wiliam Walton)

Concerto for Piano and Nonet (Constant Lambert)

1932

Politics

MARCH

Tariff of 10% imposed on majority of imports.

APRIL

Tariffs on manufactures increased to 20% or more.

AUGUST

Imperial preference agreed by conference in Ottawa.

SEPTEMBER

Philip Snowden resigns from government with Free Trade Liberals (including Lord Samuel) in protest against protectionism.

OCTOBER

Foundation of British Union of Fascists.

Town & Country Planning Act.

Ray Report ends free secondary schooling.

Architecture

Arnos Grove Station (Charles Holden)

Broadcasting House (Val Myer, with interiors by McGrath, Coates, Chermayeff etc)

White House, Haslemere (Connell & Ward)

Boots D10 ('Wets') building, Nottingham (Sir Owen Williams)

High Cross House, Dartington (William Lescaze)

Royal Corinthian Yacht Club, Burnham-on-Crouch (Joseph Emberton)

Shakespeare Memorial Theatre, Stratford-on-Avon (Scott, Chesteron & Shepherd)

Modern Architecture International Exhibition, MOMA, New York.

Design

Design in Industry magazine (DIA)

Room and Book (Paul Nash)

Foley China (decorated by Paul Nash, Laura Knight, Vanessa Bell etc.)

Competition for design of Ekco Radios.

Gorrell Report on Art and Industry.

Literature/Music/Film

Brave New World (Aldous Huxley)

The Orators (W H Auden)

1933

Politics

JANUARY

Hitler becomes German chancellor.

APRIL

Anglo-German trade agreement.

Art

Formation of Unit One.

Art Now (Herbert Read)

Architecture

Gorilla house, London Zoo (Lubetkin & Tecton)

The Hopfield, St Mary's Platt, Kent (Colin Lucas)

Midland Hotel, Morecambe (Oliver Hill)

Formation of MARS Group.

Design

Exhibition of British Industrial Art in Relation to the Home (Dorland Hall). Council for Art and industry formed.

Literature/Music/Film

The Private Life of Henry VIII (Alexander Korda)

1934

Politics

FEBRUARY

Anglo-Soviet trade agreement.

Art

Unit One exhibition at Mayor Gallery, with book.

White Reliefs (Ben Nicholson)

Architecture

Lawn Road Flats (Wells Coates)

Sassoon House, Peckham (Maxwell Fry)

Torilla, Hatfield (F R S Yorke)

Caveman Restaurant (Geoffrey Jellicoe and Russell Page)

Royal Masonic Hospital, Ravenscourt Park (Burnet, Tait & Lorne)

Sunspan House (Wells Coates) exhibited at Ideal Home Exhibition.

Walter Gropius and Eric Mendelsohn settle in England.

Modernismus, a study (Sir Reginald Blomfield)

Design

Art and Industry (Herbert Read)

Exhibition of Contemporary Industrial Design in the Home (Dorland Hall).

Literature/Music/Film

New Verse magazine.

Frost in May (Antonia White)

I Claudius , Claudius the God (Robert Graves)

Song of Ceylon (Basil Wright)

Music Ho! a study of music in decline (Constant Lambert)

Death of Sir Edward Elgar and Gustav Holst.

1935

Politics

JANUARY – FEBRUARY

Unemployment Assistance Board crisis.

MAY

Celebration of Silver Jubilee of King George V.

JUNE

Resignation of Ramsay MacDonald, succeeded by Stanley Baldwin.

OCTOBER

Italy attacks Abyssinia.

Art

Artists's International Association.

Axis magazine.

A Short Survey of Surrealism (David Gascoyne).

Final exhibition of the Seven and Five Society.

Architecture

Peckham Health Centre (Sir Owen Williams)

Highpoint I (Lubetkin & Tecton)

Embassy Court, Brighton (Wells Coates)

Pullman Court flats, Streatham
(Frederick Gibberd)

Kensal House flats (Maxwell Fry)

London Gliding Club, Dunstable
(Christopher Nicholson)

De la Warr Pavilion, Bexhill-on-Sea
(Mendelsohn & Chermayeff)

Quarry Hill flats, Leeds
(R A H Livett, finished 1941)

Marcel Breuer settles in England.

Design

British Art in Industry Exhibition,
Royal Academy.

SS *Orion* (Brian O'Rorke for Orient Line).

Signature magazine.

László Moholy-Nagy settles in England.

Literature/Film/Music

Some Versions of Pastoral (William Empson)

The Green Child (Herbert Read)

Sweeny Agonistes (T S Eliot)

Murder in the Cathedral (T S Eliot)

The Dog Beneath the Skin
(Auden and Isherwood)

The Thirty-Nine Steps (Alfred Hitchcock)

Colour Box (Len Lye)

Housing Problems (Arthur Elton)

Coalface (Alberto Cavalcanti)

Things to Come (Alexander Korda)

Symphony in B flat minor, N° 1
(Willam Walton)

Symphony in F minor, No.4
(Ralph Vaughan Williams)

String Quartet No. 1 - first version
(Michael Tippett)

1936

Politics

JANUARY

Death of King George V.

JULY

Outbreak of Spanish Civil War.

OCTOBER

Battle of Cable Street between British
Union of Fascists and protestors.

DECEMBER

Abdication of King Edward VIII, succeeded
by King George VI. Public order Act bans
wearing of political uniforms.

Art

International Surrealist Exhibition

Architecture

Sun House, Frognal Way, Hampstead,
(Maxwell Fry)

Whittinghame College, Brighton
(A V Pilichowski)

Simpson's, Piccadilly (Joseph Emberton)

St Ann's Hill (Raymond McGrath)

Peter Jones (William Crabtree with Slater &
Moberley and Sir Charles Reilly)

The City of the Future (project, Yorke &
Breuer) Gane Show House, Bristol
(Yorke & Breuer)

64 Old Church Street
(Mendelsohn & Chermayeff)

62 Old Church Street (Gropius & Fry)

Design

Isokon Long Chair and Short Chair
(Marcel Breuer)

Pioneers of the Modern Movement
(Nikolaus Pevsner)

RIBA 'Exhibition of Everyday Things'

Literature/Film/Music

Left Book Club founded by Victor Gollancz.
Peak membership of 60,000.

The Ascent of F6 (Auden and Isherwood)

Night Mail (Harry Watt)

Our Hunting Fathers (Benjamin Britten)

1937

Politics

APRIL

New Indian constitution comes into force.

MAY

Coronation of King George VI. Baldwin
resigns as Prime Minister, succeeded by
Neville Chamberlain.

Art

Painting 1937 (Ben Nicholson)

Circle

Foundation of Euston Road School

Colour and Form (Adrian Stokes)

Art and Society (Herbert Read)

Contemporary Lithographs (founded by
John Piper and Robert Wellington)

Architecture

News Chronicle Schools Competition

ICI Laboratories, Blackley
(Serge Chermayeff)

Modern Architecture in England
Exhibition, MOMA, New York.

How we celebrate the Coronation
(Robert Byron)

Gropius and Breuer leave for USA.

Design

Paris International Exhibition

Enquiry into Industrial Art in Britain
(Nikolaus Pevsner)

Literature/Film/Music

The Years (Virginia Woolf)

Homage to Catalonia (George Orwell)

Letters from Iceland (Auden and MacNeice)

Continual Dew (John Betjeman)

First Symphony (Edmund Rubbra)

Mass Observation founded.

1938

Politics

MARCH

Austria annexed by Germany

SEPTEMBER

Munich Conference, Neville Chamberlain
accepts German annexation of
Sudetenland.

OCTOBER

Resignation of Duff Cooper as First Lord of
the Admiralty in protest at Munich
Agreeement.

Art

Recumbent Figure (Henry Moore)

High Street (Eric Ravilious)

The Principles of Art (R G Collingwood)

Mondrian settles in London.

Architecture

Finsbury Health Centre (Lubetkin & Tecton)

Highpoint II (Lubetkin & Tecton)

Richmond Girls' High School (Denis Clarke-Hall)

Bentley Wood, Sussex (Serge Chermayeff)

Nursery School, Northwich, Cheshire (Martin & Speight)

32 Newton Road, Paddington (Denys Lasdun)

MARS Group Exhibition, New Burlington Galleries.

Focus magazine founded.

Design

Design (Anthony Bertam).

Literature/Film/Music

Brighton Rock (Graham Greene)

Collected Poems (C Day Lewis)

Murphy (Samuel Beckett)

Enemies of Promise (Cyril Connolly)

The Marxist Philosophy and the Sciences (J B S Haldane)

Variations on a Theme of Frank Bridge (Benjamin Britten)

Picture Post founded.

1939

Politics

MARCH

German invasion of Czechoslovakia.

APRIL

Hitler denounces Anglo-German naval agreement. Conscription introduced.

SEPTEMBER

German invasion of Poland. Declaration of war on 3 September. Evacuation of civilian women and children from large cities.

Art

Living Art in England, London Gallery.

Brighton Aquatints (John Piper).

Ben Nicholson and Barbara Hepworth move to Cornwall (25 August).

Architecture

1-3 Willow Road, Hampstead (Ernö Goldfinger)

Impington Village College (Gropius & Fry)

Harbour Meadow, Bosham (Moro & Llewelyn Davies)

All-Europe House (Elizabeth Denby) exhibited at Ideal Home Exhibition.

Design

The Flat Book (Martin & Speight)

Literature/Film/Music

Finnegan's Wake (James Joyce)

Autumn Journal (Louis MacNeice)

The Social Function of Science (J D Bernal)

Spare Time (Humphrey Jennings)

Les Illuminations (Benjamin Britten)

Violin Concerto (William Walton)

Dies Natalis (Gerald Finzi)

Publishing credits:

Produced by:

Turner Libros S.A.

Zurbano, 10. 2º
28010 Madrid

Designed by:

Leslie Levy

Printed in Spain

Published by:

Design Museum

Shad Thames
London SE1 2YD
T 0171 403 69 33
F 0171 378 65 40

ISBN: 1-872005-39-X   327039

D.L.: M-677-1999

© 1999 Design Museum and the authors

On the cover:
De La Warr Pavilion, Bexhill-on-Sea,
Mendelsohn & Chermayeff.
Photograph: John Riddy, 1998.
Courtesy of Frith Street Gallery, London.

On page 4:
H S Goodhart-Rendel, Hay's Wharf,
North elevation, 1929. Watercolour.
British Architectural Library, RIBA, London.

On page 137:
Graham Sutherland, *Entrance to a Lane*, 1939.
Oil on canvas.
The Trustees of the Tate Gallery, London.

MODERN BRITAIN 1929-1939

PRINTED AND BOUND IN MADRID

JANUARY 1999